NEW DIRECTIONS FOR TEACHING AND LEARNING

Robert J. Menges, *Northwestern University*
EDITOR-IN-CHIEF

Marilla D. Svinicki, *University of Texas, Austin*
ASSOCIATE EDITOR

Approaches to Teaching Non-Native English Speakers Across the Curriculum

David L. Sigsbee
Bruce W. Speck
Bruce Maylath
University of Memphis

EDITORS

Number 70, Summer 1997

JOSSEY-BASS PUBLISHERS
San Francisco

APPROACHES TO TEACHING NON-NATIVE ENGLISH SPEAKERS
ACROSS THE CURRICULUM
David L. Sigsbee, Bruce W. Speck, Bruce Maylath (eds.)
New Directions for Teaching and Learning, no. 70
Robert J. Menges, Editor-in-Chief
Marilla D. Svinicki, Associate Editor

Microfilm copies of issues and articles are available in 16mm and 35mm, as well as microfiche in 105mm, through University Microfilms Inc., 300 North Zeeb Road, Ann Arbor, Michigan 48106-1346.

ISSN 0271-0633   ISBN 0-7879-9860-5

NEW DIRECTIONS FOR TEACHING AND LEARNING is part of The Jossey-Bass Higher and Adult Education Series and is published quarterly by Jossey-Bass Inc., Publishers, 350 Sansome Street, San Francisco, California 94104-1342. Periodicals postage paid at San Francisco, California, and at additional mailing offices. POSTMASTER: Send address changes to New Directions for Teaching and Learning, Jossey-Bass Inc., Publishers, 350 Sansome Street, San Francisco, California 94104-1342.

New Directions for Teaching and Learning is indexed in College Student Personnel Abstracts, Contents Pages in Education, and Current Index to Journals in Education (ERIC).

SUBSCRIPTIONS cost $52.00 for individuals and $79.00 for institutions, agencies, and libraries. Prices subject to change.

EDITORIAL CORRESPONDENCE should be sent to the editor-in-chief, Robert J. Menges, Northwestern University, Center for the Teaching Professions, 2115 North Campus Drive, Evanston, Illinois 60208-2610.

Cover photograph by Richard Blair/Color & Light © 1990.

Jossey-Bass Web address: http://www.josseybass.com

Manufactured in the United States of America on Lyons Falls Pathfinder Tradebook. This paper is acid-free and 100 percent totally chlorine-free.

CONTENTS

FROM THE SERIES EDITORS

About This Publication. Since 1980, *New Directions for Teaching and Learning (NDTL)* has brought a unique blend of theory, research, and practice to leaders in postsecondary education. *NDTL* sourcebooks strive not only for solid substance but also for timeliness, compactness, and accessibility.

The series has four goals: to inform readers about current and future directions in teaching and learning in postsecondary education, to illuminate the context that shapes these new directions, to illustrate these new directions through examples from real settings, and to propose ways in which these new directions can be incorporated into still other settings.

This publication reflects our view that teaching deserves respect as a high form of scholarship. We believe that significant scholarship is conducted not only by researchers who report results of empirical investigations but also by practitioners who share disciplined reflections about teaching. Contributors to *NDTL* approach questions of teaching and learning as seriously as they approach substantive questions in their own disciplines, and they deal not only with pedagogical issues but also with the intellectual and social context in which these issues arise. Authors deal on the one hand with theory and research and on the other with practice, and they translate from research and theory to practice and back again.

About This Volume. More and more students at American colleges and universities do not have English as their first language. Others have learned a version of English that is significantly different from how Americans speak and write. The consequences for oral and written communication are frustrating for students and teachers. This issue of *New Directions for Teaching and Learning* is intended for teachers in any field who work with these students but who are neither linguists nor specialists in English as a second language. Contributors suggest how teachers can shape instruction—through class discussions, small group work, out-of-class assignments, and feedback to students—in ways that strengthen students' communication skills.

Robert J. Menges, *Editor-in-Chief*
Marilla D. Svinicki, *Associate Editor*

ORDERING INFORMATION

NEW DIRECTIONS FOR TEACHING AND LEARNING is a series of paperback books that presents ideas and techniques for improving college teaching, based both on the practical expertise of seasoned instructors and on the latest research findings of educational and psychological researchers. Books in the series are published quarterly in Spring, Summer, Fall, and Winter and are available for purchase by subscription as well as by single copy.

SUBSCRIPTIONS cost $52.00 for individuals (a savings of 35 percent over single-copy prices) and $79.00 for institutions, agencies, and libraries. Please do not send institutional checks for personal subscriptions. Standing orders are accepted. Prices subject to change. (For subscriptions outside of North America, add $7.00 for shipping via surface mail or $25.00 for air mail. Orders *must be prepaid* in U.S. dollars by check drawn on a U.S. bank or charged to VISA, MasterCard, or American Express.)

SINGLE COPIES cost $20.00 plus shipping (see below) when payment accompanies order. California, New Jersey, New York, and Washington, D.C., residents please include appropriate sales tax. Canadian residents add GST and any local taxes. Billed orders will be charged shipping and handling. No billed shipments to post office boxes. (Orders from outside North America *must be prepaid* in U.S. dollars by check drawn on a U.S. bank or charged to VISA, MasterCard, or American Express.)

SHIPPING (SINGLE COPIES ONLY): $20.00 and under, add $3.50; to $50.00, add $4.50; to $75.00, add $5.50; to $100.00, add $6.50; to $150.00, add $7.50; over $150.00, add $8.50.

DISCOUNTS FOR QUANTITY ORDERS are available. Please write to the address below for information.

ALL ORDERS must include either the name of an individual or an official purchase order number. Please submit your order as follows:
   Subscriptions: specify series and year subscription is to begin
   Single copies: include individual title code (such as TL54)

MAIL ALL ORDERS TO:
   Jossey-Bass Publishers
   350 Sansome Street
   San Francisco, CA 94104-1342

FOR SUBSCRIPTION SALES OUTSIDE OF THE UNITED STATES, CONTACT:
   any international subscription agency or Jossey-Bass directly.

EDITORS' NOTES

An advertisement on a campus bulletin board began with the sentence "Math is an easy pie for you to get." The ad continued reassuringly, "A lot of students get 'A's on the courses they failed and treat like headache when they get my assistance." The ad was probably posted by an international student who was quite skillful in math but for whom English was a second language.

A typical college professor approaching such language in a student's paper would probably not know where to begin with corrections. Should the badly used idioms "easy pie for you to get" and "treat like headache" be corrected first? What about the verb tense problems in "they failed and treat"? Or should he or she focus on the word order in "treat like headache when they get my assistance"? The reaction of many of us who teach at colleges and universities is either to give up and blame the student's English instructors for this kind of writing or to correct begrudgingly all of the errors as we suppose an English teacher would. As you will see in the chapters of this volume, other approaches produce better results.

Who Are the Students?

Many kinds of students in American universities use English as a second language or as a foreign language, and they are referred to in a variety of ways. They may be called "international students" or "foreign students," even though those are very general terms that can include students from English-speaking countries. In fact, some of them may be students who are native speakers of English, but not of American English. At other times they are referred to as ESL students, a term derived from the fact that many of them take special English as a Second Language classes.

There is such a variety of students, and their levels of intent about learning and using English successfully are so multifarious, that no easily constructed set of terms can be applied to them. In this volume we have attempted to simplify the terminology by commonly referring to them, whenever possible, as *non-native* speakers, as *non-native* writers of English, or as *English-as-a-second-language* writers, written in lower case. The term *English as a Second Language,* written with capital letters, and the abbreviation *ESL* are only used to refer to the academic discipline whose specialists teach in the subject area *English as a Second Language.* Whatever the terminological issues may be, understanding the variety of non-native speakers and writers in your classroom is critical to effective teaching. Every reader of this volume should begin with Stalker's chapter "My Language, My Culture: International Variations in Standards for English," which gives an extended description of the types of non-native students.

What Teachers Can Do

Although in many cases you can send non-native students with language problems to experts in your English department or to a campus writing center, in specific cases you may wish to deal with some of their problems yourself. If the issue is related to particular and idiosyncratic styles of your discipline, a considerable part of the burden *must* fall on your shoulders. However, in this role as a content-area expert you may have difficulty determining which errors are serious and which are not. Your difficulty in dealing with language problems may be compounded by cultural issues, but you may not know what those issues are. For instance, because of different cultural assumptions, your American students and your international students sometimes do not work together well on group writing projects. You may attempt to address these cultural differences in an informal setting by inviting students to your home, yet some of the international students do not come, or they stay for a time but appear uncomfortable and leave early.

Goal of This Volume

The goal of this volume is to guide faculty in subject areas other than English so that they can deal effectively and appropriately with the writing and speaking styles of their students who are non-native users of English or who have learned a variant of English different from what Americans use. As such, this is written in a direct and nontechnical style to make it as available and useful as possible. It is designed not only to give advice and direction on how and when to work on students' writing and speaking but also to give counsel and caveats on when to turn problems over to a specialist in English as a Second Language.

The authors who provide this information come from distinguished and varied backgrounds. They represent and combine expertise in a number of areas including English as a Second Language instruction, composition theory, editing, technical writing, interpersonal communication, oral communication, and linguistics. All are practitioners as well as theorists and recognize the need to present the practical results of their findings to an audience of teachers and others who are not experts in ESL communication issues.

Overview of the Contents

The volume is arranged so that the opening chapters define and discuss broad issues related to language and culture, and the later chapters deal with more particular issues of application and problem solving. This design creates coherence for the whole work, but each chapter is written so that it can be read independently. The following detailed summaries provide an overview of content and make clear the relationship between chapters.

In Chapter One, "My Language, My Culture: International Variations in Standards for English," Stalker provides examples showing how international variations in English affect communication. He notes that although students may have studied English, this does not mean that they have studied American or British English. In fact, they may have learned an international variety of English, such as Malaysian or Turkish English. In such cases what you regard as an error may be an acceptable construction according to the students' international variety of English. In any case, it is important for us as teachers who grade students' writing to respond to written language as we do spoken language—look first at content. Finally, the quality of students' English and their performance may be restricted by personal and cultural issues that limit the level of proficiency they intend to achieve.

In Chapter Two, "Which Non-Native Speaker? Differences Between International Students and U.S. Resident (Language Minority) Students," Reid extends the distinctions made by Stalker. She explains that it is not enough simply to say that a student is a non-native speaker or writer. Careful distinctions must be made, for instance, between students who are literate in their first language and those who are not. Some students first learn English in the classroom, whereas others learn it by listening. Students from this latter group are frequently U.S. residents (for example, former refugees) who are orally fluent but will have to unlearn and relearn many rules to prepare themselves for academic writing. In all cases, it is imperative for teachers to evaluate errors as they affect understanding and to put primary emphasis on corrections that improve clarity.

In Chapter Three, "Why Do They Get It When I Say 'Gingivitis' But Not When I Say 'Gum Swelling'?" Maylath describes in broad terms how a student's native language and culture can influence his or her understanding of English vocabulary in unanticipated ways. For example, students who speak a Romance language may not understand Anglo-Saxon-based English vocabulary, but they may be quite sophisticated in their understanding of Greek- and Latin-based English technical vocabulary. This can happen because English technical terms share many common etymological elements with the students' native languages. In addition to vocabulary problems, common obstacles students encounter include idiomatic language and unexpected connotations of words. Students also sometimes become hyperfluent; that is, they overuse Greek- and Latin-based words for prestige reasons. There are strategies and resources both the teacher and the student can use to deal with these issues.

In Chapter Four, "Respect for Religious Differences: The Case of Muslim Students," Speck shows that through knowledge of the cultural restrictions that influence and limit student actions, a teacher can create a comfortable learning environment for non-native students. Muslim students constitute a good example of students in American classrooms whose behavior and religious practices may be misunderstood. And this misunderstanding may be compounded by the students' inability to elaborate and explain their perspectives in English. Through a series of interviews, Muslim students define the problems from their perspectives and offer solutions, all of which can give teachers insights into the students' worldview.

In Chapter Five, "Cultural Norms Affect Oral Communication in the Classroom," Johnson explains how broader cultural issues influence the way students conduct themselves in whole-class interaction, small-group interaction, and class presentations. For example, some societies encourage a reluctance to display one's knowledge, whereas others allow and even expect individuals to express their views forthrightly and to make independent interpretations. From another perspective, in some societies people rely heavily on the context of a situation for meaning, but in others (U.S. society among them), people require clarity and specificity to determine meaning and put far less emphasis on context. Teachers need to understand such cultural factors in order to facilitate all students' contributions to a class and to avoid underestimating students' intellectual abilities and learning levels in classroom interactions.

In Chapter Six, "Using the 'Writing Process' with Non-Native Users of English," Koffolt and Holt provide specific details for using the "writing process" with non-native writers. All students benefit when their teachers direct the writing process, but for non-native writers there are special considerations, as some errors may arise from not knowing the conventions of American academic writing style. Teachers can help students by using a process model, in which they guide the gathering of ideas, drafting, revising, and editing, with feedback given at appropriate points. This procedure has special advantages for non-native writers because it also provides opportunities to learn the academic style appropriate to a given discipline. Finally, such students will benefit greatly from feedback and discussions with peers before they prepare a paper for final submission.

In Chapter Seven, "Building Editing Skills: Putting Students at the Center of the Editing Process," Murie turns to the particulars of helping non-native writers with language-related issues by putting the student, not the teacher, at the center of the editing process. The goal is to help students identify their trouble spots while still retaining control over the editing process. The role of the teacher is to be a resource to the student by guiding the editing process, understanding student perceptions, and using effective techniques, which include conferencing.

In Chapter Eight, "Responding to Grammar Errors," Holt deals with specific types of errors and error correction. She observes that the method of correcting a paper by carefully marking all errors and giving a grade that reflects an evaluation of grammar skills is not effective with non-native students. Content-area teachers need to realize that their task is not merely to correct grammar but to help students become writers in an academic field. They can do this by looking at content first, concentrating on problems that interfere with understanding, and by allowing for revisions. Holt then provides an overview of typical errors, strategies for dealing with them, and advice on when to send a student to the ESL experts for help.

In Chapter Nine, "How Cultural Differences Affect Written and Oral Communication: The Case of Peer Response Groups," Nelson brings together the topics of writing and oral communication with strategies for dealing with problems arising from cultural differences. Peer response groups can help students become better writers and can help faculty by reducing the amount of error to be corrected in papers. But particular problems arise because American students and non-native students may view the purpose of group work differently, and thus groups made up of both types of students do not always work effectively. An examination of this problem from the perspective of interpersonal communications provides insights into how different groups work and suggests ways to structure groups for maximum effectiveness.

In Chapter Ten, "Please Speak Up: Asian Immigrant Students in American College Classrooms," Hodne examines non-native students' oral communication problems from a practical point of view. Asian students report that they find that their academic load is heavy, they have cultural adaptation problems, and they have insufficient opportunities to communicate with American students. Some also feel that changing their speech style to an American model may force them to give up their language identity. Both American and Asian students need to be coached on communication styles and strategies so that they can learn to communicate effectively among themselves and learn the styles of academic discourse appropriate to their fields. By making use of informal conversations and structured opportunities for oral communication, faculty can manage the classroom in a way that leads both groups to use classroom talk to rehearse academic language skills.

In Chapter Eleven, "What Teachers Can Do to Relieve Problems Identified by International Students," Lee draws together many issues raised throughout the book by combining teachers' concerns with student perspectives on non-native language issues. Lee shows how students view many of the issues raised in earlier chapters and provides her own response to the problems students define. She reports that one specific group of students identified and provided solutions to the following problem areas: listening ability, differences in cultural background, oral communication skills, vocabulary, and writing. Although the solutions proposed are not always practical, they provide a guide for teachers about issues that students see as difficult or sensitive.

Acknowledgments

On behalf of the authors of this volume we want to thank the many subject-area faculty who user-tested various drafts of the chapters. Their criticisms and encouragement have been invaluable in helping us to bring the most useful topics together and to address the intended audience.

Most especially thanks are due to Martha J. Payne, who applied her substantial editorial and copyediting skills to this volume. Much of the clarity in both form and content is due to her efforts, and only with the greatest difficulty could we have completed this project without her.

DAVID L. SIGSBEE is a faculty member in the Department of Foreign Languages and Literatures at the University of Memphis. He is also director of the university's general education program, for which he oversees faculty development activities.

BRUCE W. SPECK is an associate professor of English at the University of Memphis, where he is coordinator of the writing-across-the-curriculum program.

BRUCE MAYLATH is an assistant professor of English in the Department of English at the University of Memphis. He teaches in the Professional and Technical Writing program. He has taught ESL in Michigan and English as a Foreign Language in Norway.

"Errors" in international students' writing often surprise us. These "errors" may persist because students want to retain their variety of English and their cultural identity.

My Language, My Culture: International Variations in Standards for English

James C. Stalker

International students come to our classes with a language different from our own and with multiple purposes for their use of English, and we come to our classes with our own expectations about English and about foreign students' abilities in English. We assume that international students have had English instruction, usually sufficient for them to undertake an academic program in English. However, we know that most students do not enter their academic classes with full fluency in English, so for them, inevitably, an academic class is an English class as well as a chemistry or math or political science class. When we see language "errors" in the students' papers, this dual nature of our classes is brought to our attention and can lead to frustration. Some of us wonder why these students were allowed to take academic classes and place extra demands on us. Others of us feel obliged to help the non-native speakers improve their English but are not sure how. We can reduce the level of our frustration and perhaps take a more productive approach for us and the students if we reconsider a couple of our assumptions about students' language and why they use it the way they do.

For instance, language features that differ from our own are not always errors. Although American English is widely used around the world, it is not *the* international standard. Accepted standards of English vary from country to country, and those variations will appear in our students' writing. These variations are not errors; they are simply part of a different international variety of English. When international students' writing does not meet our linguistic expectations, we may judge the writing inadequate because we regard the language as flawed, as bad English. Sometimes it is. Sometimes students do not

New Directions for Teaching and Learning, no. 70, Summer 1997 © Jossey-Bass Publishers

know what they want to say, and the language reflects that. But often the language is just different.

We also need to recognize that a lack of improvement in language use over the semester does not always indicate an inability to learn English. Of course, failure to improve may be the result of inadequate intellectual capacity or lack of desire, but it is also likely that limitations on accuracy and fluency may result from personal and cultural restrictions rather than from linguistic inability. Students may not see a need to adopt our American English because they know that they will be returning to their home country and their home standards. It is also true that some cultures indirectly let students know that "too much English" is not a good thing.

What do we do about these differences and restrictions? How can we possibly know what is a legitimate variation and what is an error, or which students can and will become fluent in English? Our best course is to treat written work as a communicative act rather than as a display of linguistic prowess and to respond to the communicative effectiveness of our students' work rather than to the closeness of fit to American linguistic expectations. In other words, respond to your students' written English more as you respond to their spoken English. We hear the same variations when students talk to us, but we are less likely to notice the differences because when we talk with students we are focused on content, *what* the student is saying, rather than on form, *how* the student is saying it. If we cannot understand them, we tell them so. If the communication is flawed, we ask for clarification. We should do the same with writing that we do with talking. Respond to the content, not the language, and there is a high likelihood that the language will alter to more nearly approach our expectations. (See Holt's chapter for strategies for this approach, and Johnson's for a discussion of differences in rhetorical formats.)

International Standards and Varieties

We often assume that the English of our international students, however halting, is either Standard American or British English. However, students bring a range of international varieties of English to the classroom. These include varieties that are generally recognized outside the United States as legitimate international varieties of English, for example, Malaysian or Nigerian English. In countries where England had a long and strong institutional presence during their colonial period, local varieties of English developed, and they continued to develop in the postcolonial era into distinct varieties. It is important to note that these varieties are not a language mix, a patois or a creole, but variants of British English. It is also important to recognize that most of these countries have substantial populations of native speakers of the local variety of English. India, for example, has about 75 million native speakers of English, approximately four times as many more than in all of Canada. The English they speak is Indian English, based on British English, but a separate international variety of English. These 75 million people may indeed speak a second, local language, Hindi perhaps, but English is their first, their native language. Other countries that fall into this category are Puerto Rico, Pakistan, Uganda, Kenya, South Africa, Zambia, Swaziland, Zimbabwe, Sudan, Tanzania, Ivory Coast, Ghana, Sierra Leone, Bangladesh, Burma, Philippines, Hong Kong, Singapore, French Guiana, Guyana, and Surinam.

Other students come to us with English varieties that are noticeably influenced by the students' native language; they are speakers of English as a second language, usually American or British English, but with a national character. Such varieties include Japanese English, Turkish English, or Brazilian English. These students' first language, their native language, is one of the indigenous languages of their home country. We cannot always tell by listening or reading whether a student is a native speaker of an international variety of English or whether English is a second language. This is especially true of students from a country like India where there are both native and non-native speakers of English and there are apparent similarities in their speech. Problems arise in either case when we correct features that appear to be wrong but are in fact normal features in the students' usual variety of English. Such corrections lose our own and the students' valuable time in focusing their attention on features of their writing that can be adjusted later. The students can get confused because they simply do not understand what the problem is. After all, the teacher has marked something that they know is not wrong!

Variation in American English

To gain some perspective on the international variation we can expect to find in the classroom, we will look first at an example or two of variation within American English. We often assume a level of consistency in American English that does not exist. We also assume that our American students' English falls within the accepted range of standard. As a result, we often do not notice their unusual uses, uses that when highlighted we might well regard as "nonstandard" or even "foreign" if found on a paper with a foreign name. The focus here is not such nonprestige variations as *ain't* and double negatives but rather subtler shifts in use. For example, as native users of English, we worry little about our prepositions. Their use is consistent and predictable. But some examples of the use of *of* might be enlightening. After each sentence in the following examples, the source is in parentheses, and the preposition one might expect is in brackets:

1. Dysfunctional: used in reference *of* families which are unable to function normally. (student paper) [*to*]
2. Gilda was possessed *of* the spirit of the theater. (local newspaper) [*by* or *with*]
3. The festival will boast *of* such musical acts as the Bangles, Smokey Robinson, the Nylons and Lee Greenwood on the main stage. (student newspaper) [no preposition]

4. "The movie company sent out requests *of* Civil War re-enactors around the U.S. asking if they would like to be in the movie," Maynard said. (student newspaper) [*for*]
5. The Bon in Shanghai is one example of the impressive architecture that hints *of* Shanghai's opulent past. (major airline in-flight magazine) [*at*]

Only one of these examples is from an unpublished source. The remainder are published examples; therefore, they can be regarded as acceptable educated standard usage. It is highly unlikely that we would notice these variant uses of *of* in an American student's paper and probably not at all likely in published sources. At most, we might think, "Gee, I wouldn't use *of* that way," and read on. Our expectation that these writers (student or professional) are native writers of English leads us to ignore such variations or to accord them little importance.

International student writers will not necessarily benefit from that same assumption. We will likely be more highly sensitive to such variation in their writing than in our American students' writing. Some research indicates that the difference between non-native speakers' unusual preposition use and native speakers' unusual preposition use is one of frequency rather than kind (Stalker and Stalker, 1988). That is, both native and non-native writers will use *of* (and other prepositions) when we expect a different preposition, but native writers' use will be at a lower frequency than non-native writers' use.

Contrasts Between British and American English

It is highly likely that the international kind of English students have been taught will be British rather than American English. This is certainly the case in countries where there has been a long-term British presence, and it even occurs in countries like Japan where there has been a long-term, strong American influence. In part, the persistence of British English in the world of English language pedagogy is a function of the availability of texts and the interest of the British government in promoting the British variety of English. British English language texts are readily available around the world; American texts have been more difficult to get and are therefore less used. Through the British Council, the British government actively and avidly promotes the teaching and learning of British English (using British texts). The American government has only a handful of English Language Officers around the world who, though active, are no match for the British. As a result, students learn British English and, as a further consequence, bring their British English with them to their American schools.

Most of us assume that British and American English are quite close in structure; after all, British and American English are mother and daughter and in constant, close contact. They are clearly mutually intelligible. They are the two most studied of the international dialects of English. Whichever you learn, it will travel well. But a few illustrations will demonstrate that from an American perspective there are surprises even in British English. To continue our prepositional focus through several more examples, readers of British novels (or viewers of British shows on PBS or Arts & Entertainment) know that a British resident lives *in* Milford Street, whereas an American resident lives *on* Milford Street. In a similar vein, when we are asked to call someone in British English, we will call them *on* 800–555–1212 rather than *at* 800–555–1212. An even more noticeable example of odd preposition use, from an American perspective, appeared in an issue of *The Economist*: "If the talks succeed, Peru will be the last of the Latin American defaulters to agree such a scheme" ("The Last of the Brady Bunch," 1995, p. 89). On an American student's paper, many of us would assume that the missing preposition was just an oversight; it is so odd. On an international student's paper, we are more likely to assume that the student is not fully fluent in English, when in fact the student is using perfectly acceptable British English.

Another example of a pervasive and subtle British structural difference is the use of -*ing* verbs (a sign that reads "Turning Ahead") where Americans would use the simple verb ("Turn Ahead") or an entirely different syntactic structure. For example, British English "Our opening times are 9:30 to 5:30" would most comfortably become American English "We are open 9:30 to 5:30." Likewise, "Check that you have dialing tone" would necessarily be translated as "Listen for a dial tone" in American English. And one final example, "Call us on 900 200 quoting reference no. S74" would more likely be "Call 900 200 to order item no. S74."

If we know that we are reading British English, we expect differences but expect to be able to comprehend the text, and make the appropriate perceptual and psychological adjustments to allow that comprehension to happen. Those adjustments are quite significant, because as we can see from the examples, British and American English can be quite different, more so than we often suppose, but we read with the assumption that we will mostly be able to understand the text. Similar sorts of differences in international students' writing may lead us to assume a lack of knowledge of English on the writer's part and to make a consequent assumption that the text will be difficult to understand. The more accurate assumption would be the same one we make for British English; namely, the writer's English is different, but not necessarily deficient or incomprehensible.

Other International Standards

International students will bring some of these British features to their writing, and their writing is also likely to include features that are locally acceptable, features that teachers in the native country tolerate or do not even notice. As a result, students will assume that they are writing "correct" English, accurate English, whereas we may conclude that the students' English is not very good, interpreting the local or international standard features as "not English." The following examples come from the two kinds of international English discussed earlier. The first set of examples is taken from Malaysian English, a variety of English that has a long history of use in a country in which English is not the majority language, but that has native-born users for whom the local variety of English is their native language, a *nativized* variety of English (Kachru, 1986). The second set is from Turkish English, which is a second language for the user but contains characteristics that are commonly used by many, or even most, of the users of English in that country.

Malaysian English. For Americans, nouns such as *attendance, lettuce,* and *entertainment* do not have plurals with an s. We do not say or write *attendances.* For Malaysian English users, all have plurals with -s. (All the Malaysian examples are taken from McKay, 1993.) A native user of Malaysian English will say and write, "The *entertainments* were very mixed in quality," meaning what an American means by "The *acts* were very mixed in quality." They will also use "My students' *attendances* are quite good this semester." In fact, variation in what we accept as a legitimate plural is quite common around the world. For example, the plural of *research* seems to be *researches* in most international variants of English, except American English.

Acceptable verb use varies as well. Malaysian students are likely to say and to write, "That way the forms would be *filled* and processed within minutes, rather than have the passengers *fill up* all the details while at the check point." Americans would be likely to use *out* after both instances of *fill* (or *in* after the second). Malaysian students will also say and write, "With three days before acceptance, the battle for Umno Youth Exco seats is *hotting up,*" a use we might hear in the United States, but only in jest, and only in certain regions of the country.

Our possible familiarity with *hotting up* points to one of the problems with assessing the English of students from countries with nativized English. We cannot always tell when these are older forms of British English that have been retained or new forms that have been developed in the native country. *Hot up* in the sense of "an increase in intensity or pace" developed in England in the late nineteenth century. Although this use of *hot up* is known in the United States, Americans have not adopted the usage; British colonies did.

On the other hand, some words are obviously borrowed from native languages. Malaysian examples include the following: *gotongroyong,* a form of communal cooperation; *adat,* a body of traditional law; and *rotan,* a rattan cane used for official punishment. From a Malaysian English speaker's viewpoint, whether *hot up* or *rotan* is natively British or Malaysian is irrelevant; these words and other features have become standard in Malaysian English. In the same sense, for us it makes little difference whether the variant feature is older British or newer colonial; it is still unfamiliar and, from our perspective, possibly not acceptable English.

Turkish English. Students from Turkey incorporate certain predictable features in their English, because they learn these features from their teachers and fellow users of English. The teachers do not set out to teach a strange English; often, they are not even aware that their use does not match British or

American use (the usual two standard reference varieties). English is so widely used and has been taught for so long in Turkey that certain features have become accepted as "standard"; Turkish speakers will correct their own English when they hear themselves speaking "bad English." Very fluent Turkish speakers of English regularly correct themselves when they say "Thank God!" The context is the same for them and us: we have heard good news when we expected to hear bad. However, in Turkish English the "correct" statement is "Thanks God!" with an -s, not "Thank God!" so they will correct themselves. Why the difference? We could do some elaborate analysis or historical digging to provide an explanation, but that would be a waste of time for most of us. What is important is that *Thanks God!* is acceptable Turkish English.

Another feature common to Turkish English is the absence of a predictable object after verbs. *Have* regularly occurs without an object in contexts such as the following:

QUESTION: Do you have your textbook with you today?
RESPONSE: Yes, I have.

Americans may say the same thing, but we are more likely to say "Yes, I do," or "Yes, I have it," a small but noticeable difference, especially when it occurs in writing. We also find preposition uses similar to the Malaysian examples. A Turkish English writer will write, "To summarize what I've been talking, the . . ." deleting the *about* that an American reader expects.

Two other examples of variation in preposition use are (1) the use of *since* where Americans would expect *for,* as in "Unrivaled worldwide reputation since more than 35 years" (from a bank advertisement in a locally published English language newspaper) and (2) the use of *until* where American readers would expect *up to,* as in "Students will fill in the blanks until number seven."

Meaning shifts occur as well, sometimes because of the influence of the native language. Turkish English users will say or write, "This is my first airplane ride, and I am so *excited,*" which sounds natural enough to American ears, but they will also say, "I have a final examination this afternoon, and I am so *excited.*" *Excited* in Turkish English means *nervous* as well as *excited,* a transference from the semantic similarities in the related Turkish words. Americans exhibit a similar conflation of meaning in *eager* and *anxious,* with *anxious* meaning both. When an American writes, "I am *anxious* to go home this Christmas," we do not assume that the thought of going home fills the writer with anxiety. We assume that the writer is *eager* to go home.

Limitations on Fluency and Accuracy

The second assumption discussed earlier, that students who are not fully fluent after years of exposure to English cannot or will not learn English, is more difficult to deal with. Clearly, many students for whom English is a second language become quite fluent, close to natively so. On the other hand, many of them take a very practical approach to their use of English: "How much English do I need to know to get by, to get done what I have to do?" Many of us function this way when we are living in a foreign country. We learn enough to get by, knowing that we will never use the language for any purpose other than buying groceries and traveling to interesting places. Many students will approach their classes with such a view, probably best summed up in the belief that "If you can understand what I say and write, even though you and I both know that it is inaccurate, nonfluent English, you can give me a grade, and I can get out of here and go home with my degree." As we all know, many of our American students take the same approach to language use.

For students whose first language is a variety of English other than American or British, we must accept that they speak and write fluent English. The problem is not that they are not fluent but that what they speak and write is not our English. It is relatively easy for these students to adjust their writing to adhere to educated American English standards. For them, the adjustment is a dialect shift, not a language shift. For them, if there is a problem, it is likely to be one of motivation. Whether they shift from their native dialect to an American one will depend entirely on how American or Indian or Malaysian they wish to be.

Both groups—native speakers of an international variety and speakers of a second language—converge in the degree to which they are willing to adjust their native dialect or become natively fluent. Some students and some cultures restrict the desirable level of fluency in English for cultural identity rather than pragmatic reasons. The restriction can be below the level of consciousness; the student is not aware of the restriction. But sometimes the student is quite conscious of the restriction, and those cases give us some insight into the problem. Although some research has been pursued in this area, particularly in spoken English, it is inconclusive. The research problem is quite simple. People are unlikely to admit that their target is less than native fluency. We may plead inability with impunity. We can be blatantly pragmatic, but we cannot overtly state our unwillingness to gain more than a "working" knowledge of the language if we also claim to want to use English as well as we can. Clearly, such claims would be contradictory. Consequently, the evidence linking cultural identity and lack of fluency still remains largely anecdotal. Two anecdotes will illustrate how conscious the personal decision to restrict the level of fluency can be and how changing or maintaining that restriction can significantly affect students' lives.

A young woman from Malaysia, whose first language was Malaysian English, came to a midwestern university to study as an undergraduate. Her peers and teachers found her variety of English to be attractive: "cute," as she described it. Because her nativized English was of some social use, she retained it (not entirely unconsciously, she admitted). However, her educational goal became the teaching of English. At that point, she decided that she needed and wanted to sound like her American undergraduate peers, and set about sounding like an American. When she told her story, it was in a "heartland" variety of American English. During a period of some two or three years, she had made two decisions, the first to remain an obvious speaker of Malaysian English, the second to be a fluent speaker of American English. She succeeded on both counts. Her instructors, English and otherwise, contributed neither to her "failure" nor her "success" in acquiring American English. She made the decision.

A second example illustrates a student's willingness to sacrifice potential economic success to maintain cultural identity. A young Chinese woman, a second-language speaker of English and a candidate in a master's program in teaching English as a Second Language, sought advice on how to prepare herself to get a job teaching English in the United States at the college level. Although her English was communicatively sufficient, it was noticeably influenced by her native language, particularly in her pronunciation. She was advised to alter her pronunciation to make it American sounding, because a very noticeably influenced Chinese English would likely lessen her chances for obtaining a job. Her response illustrates that fluency restrictions can be conscious, and strongly held. She said that she simply would not make that adjustment. She did not want to be perceived as an American, and her "native language–influenced English" allowed her to retain and display her native cultural identity.

Subtle cultural restrictions can also limit fluency. Japanese teachers of younger children lament the loss of fluency in English when their students move from private to public education in English at about twelve years old. Quite inexplicably, their students' English ability deteriorates rather than improves with further education. The key to the explanation may lie in the experiences of students who come to the United States on junior-year-abroad sorts of programs. Some of these students become quite fluent in English, but when they return home, they report that they must "unlearn" their fluency, must become more disfluent. In Japan, it seems, it is possible to speak and write English too well. The pressure of the culture, through one's peers, places restrictions on levels of fluency in English. Presumably, fluent American English implies the adoption of American cultural values, values that are not always positive from the Japanese view. Japanese students at American schools with large numbers of Japanese students will live with those societal restrictions even though they are in an American school. No matter how hard we work, they may well continue to talk and write Japanese English.

Conclusion

Those of us who are not English teachers are likely to assume that we are expected to teach English in addition to art or psychology. If we make this assumption, we will approach written texts with two potentially conflicting reader goals: to correct the English and to respond to art or psychology. Tough though it may be, the primary goal should be the second: to read for content. Treat the text as a communicative act, and only a communicative act. The English needs to be addressed only if it interferes with communication. Unless we are knowledgeable about international varieties of English, we cannot know whether the "error" we see is indeed an error or is an acceptable variant within some other variety of English. Most students will return to their native countries, and their English serves the purpose of learning and communicating while the students are in the United States, but their English will serve other purposes when the students return home. (See Reid's chapter on language minority students.) If fully fluent and accurate American English will be positively valued when the student returns home, the student will likely acquire both accuracy and fluency while in the United States. If fully fluent and accurate American English will be negatively valued when the student returns home, no amount of red ink will alter that barrier.

References

Kachru, B. *The Alchemy of English.* New York: Pergamon Press, 1986.
"The Last of the Brady Bunch." *The Economist,* Sept. 16, 1995, pp. 88–89.
McKay, S. L. "Sociocultural Factors in Teaching Composition to Pacific Rim Writers: An Overview." In M. N. Brock and L. Walters (eds.), *Teaching Composition Around the Pacific Rim: Politics and Pedagogy.* Clevedon, England: Multilingual Matters, 1993.
Stalker, J. W., and Stalker, J. C. "A Comparison of Pragmatic Accommodation of Non-Native and Native Speakers in Edited Written English." *World Englishes,* 1988, 7, 119–128.

JAMES C. STALKER is professor of English linguistics at Michigan State University. He held a Fulbright at Bilkent University in Ankara, Turkey, from 1990 to 1992, where he directed and taught in the master's level Teaching English as a Foreign Language program.

*Non-native English speakers fall into one of two groups: international
students or language minority students. This chapter distinguishes
between these two rather large groups, indicates their different writing
problems, and suggests how to identify and help each type of student.*

Which Non-Native Speaker?
Differences Between International
Students and U.S. Resident
(Language Minority) Students

Joy M. Reid

The telephone rings in my intensive English language program office: a faculty
member in engineering (or sociology or biology) says, in a voice that can range
from desperate to accusatory:

"I'm calling about a foreign student who writes like a first grader. I think
he needs work with his grammar."

Or:

"I have an Oriental student and I can't even read his writing because of
his grammar mistakes. I'm sending him over to your office for help."

Or:

"I've got a foreign student who just turned in a paper, and she can't even
use articles. How did she get through your program?"

Phone calls like these are opportunities for education; this chapter is for
those who do not phone. The purpose of this chapter is to focus on those student writing errors made by non-native speakers of English (called English-as-
a-second-language writers in this chapter) that often irritate or even offend
academic readers and graders. I draw distinctions between errors made by (1)
U.S. students for whom English is a second (or third or fourth) language and
(2) students who have come from non-English-speaking countries to study at
postsecondary institutions in the United States. Generally, these two groups of
students have learned their English differently, so their language problems have
different sources and different solutions. (See Stalker's chapter on speakers of
international varieties of English.)

NEW DIRECTIONS FOR TEACHING AND LEARNING, no. 70, Summer 1997 © Jossey-Bass Publishers

U.S. Resident (Language Minority) Writers

At one end of the continuum of non-native English speakers is the refugee student whose parents have fled political upheaval for the United States. These students are orally fluent in their first language, but due to limited or interrupted schooling, they are semiliterate or illiterate in that language. These students have learned English by being suddenly immersed in the language and culture of the United States. Specifically, they have acquired English principally through hearing: they listened, took in oral language (from teachers, television, grocery clerks), and subconsciously began to form vocabulary, grammar, and syntax rules—learning English through trial and error.

Usually, these students have been graduated from U.S. high schools, have had some tutoring—often fragmented—when they first entered school, and have been accumulating U.S. culture for a number of years. They have relatively developed English oral fluency and listening skills, and they understand the slang, the pop music, the behaviors, and the "cool" clothes of the schools they attend. But their reading skills may be hampered by limited understanding of the structures of the English language, and their writing displays the conversational, phonetic qualities of their "ear-based" language learning, as well as the use of their self-developed language "rules" that may, upon examination, prove to be overgeneralized or false. The following is a writing sample of a Vietnamese refugee student, written (in response to an article about students having jobs while in college) during her first day in a first-year university composition course. (Italicized and bolded words and phrases are discussed following the sample.)

> The main ideas of the Article is saying that **because of** working while going to School reduces the G.P.A. of students. Some of the Reasons **while** students *gettings* jobs is **because of** Advertisements and personnal luxuries that the students *needed* during School.
>
> What the Article is saying is true about students getting lower *grade* in school, while working. But if we try to put strict rules on College curriculas and *stopping* Television advertising, **it wouldn't help much**. Because almost all students know **what they're doing to themselves**. Students are *awared* of the lower grades they're getting but **there are more to it,** then just **because of** Work. I agree, that when you get a job, your *hour* of studying **reduces**. After coming home from work you *felt* tired and only wanted to put School **words** aside. I have *this* experiences in the past myself. It *does* reduced my G.P.A., but I'm not blaming it on T.V. advertising or **anything else**.

Three types of errors merit examination. The first are mistakes in inflection (for example, verb endings, singulars and plurals: note the italicized words). Some of these errors might occur because the student's first language, Vietnamese, is not as highly inflected as English, and lacks auxiliary verbs (*to be, to have, did* and *does*). Consequently, the student might question whether to add a plural *-s* to *grade,* and might not suspect that *are* is needed before *getting* in the second sentence. Additionally, even if the student had been tutored in English, the agreement of subjects and verbs, or of demonstrative pronouns (*this* and *that*) and nouns may not be a fully developed concept.

However, many of the verb tense errors probably occurred more from "ear-learning" than from first-language transference. That is, because the English verb tense system is complex—a single sentence, and certainly a single paragraph, may contain several verb tenses—and because these students have listened to the language rather than studied it, they may not recognize the mistakes. Moreover, because the mistakes they make may not have interfered with their ability to communicate orally, they may have structured rules for verb use that will seem idiosyncratic to the teacher. Think, for example, of a sentence like *The students are taken their time;* then read the Vietnamese student's paragraph aloud, listening for the slurring or dropping of verb endings, and thinking about how this student may have learned her verbs.

The second type of error occurs when students have made some vocabulary mistakes and have used some idiomatic expressions (correctly or incorrectly) that indicate their immersion in U.S. culture (see the bolded words and phrases). During a conference, the student who wrote the writing sample presented here indicated that she had never noticed the word *why,* thinking that *why* and *while* were the same word (*while*) with different meanings. ("Like lot of English words," she said.) Idioms used by this refugee student, which would be unknown to international students who have studied English as a foreign language, include "it wouldn't help much." An international student would say, "it would not help very much." Another, "what they're doing to themselves," would not occur in an international student's essay, nor would "anything else" (although an international student might write "any other reason"). And the use of "because of" is an oral insertion that would probably not be noticed in a conversation.

The third type of error is the seemingly arbitrary capitalization. When I asked the student why she capitalized "Article" and "School," she told me that she had learned that all nouns had to be capitalized. Of course, she did not know very much about nouns, but she did her best. She had later added the (correct) rule about capitalizing *I,* though she found this English rule peculiar and intimidating because capitalizing *I* made her "stand out too much" in her writing.

International Student Writers

At the opposite end of the continuum are international students who have chosen to attend postsecondary schools in the United States, in much the same way that U.S. college students spend a semester or a year "abroad." Many of these visa-holding students come from relatively privileged and well-educated backgrounds. They are literate and fluent in their first language, and they have learned English in foreign language classes. That is, they have learned English principally through their eyes, studying vocabulary, verb forms, and language rules.

These students know, understand, and can explain English grammar, and often their reading skills are substantial. Usually, however, their listening and oral skills are hampered by lack of experience, by non-native English-speaking teachers, and by the culture shock that comes from being immersed in a foreign culture, the language of which sounds different from their studied English language. Their writing skills are also limited because their prior English education has not provided opportunities to write formal compositions; rather it required them to complete exercises in written grammar or to answer reading questions in single sentences. The following is an e-mail message from a native Spanish speaker:

Dear Rolf Turner:
Thanks you in *asking* my question.
En memorian I *am study* models of regression and multivariates data for my **tessis academic** deductive in productivity and quality *just and time* in **management industrial**, (my carrer) in complexity with n variables **incidents operationals** and costs, this new study is cassual, and important help for our country chile and United States of America in potentials **management strategic.** *Before studied* T.U. industrial control my investigation in data *standars* in **control of qualyty final** in cocesa (cobre cerrillos s.a. chile) *associate* with Phelps Dodge in EEUU. I am not expert in statisticals but know ideas in mejority **methods productivity multivariates** in industries.

This sample presents three areas of language error. First, the italicized words and phrases indicate the interference of this writer's first language in vocabulary and syntax cognates, that is, words and structures that are close (but not exact) in meaning and use between Spanish and English. As an example of vocabulary problems, Spanish *en memorian* means "to remind you" in English. As an example of syntax problems, the lack of a subject in the sentence, "Before studied . . ." demonstrates the transference of Spanish grammar rules into English, as Spanish allows a subject not to be named if the subject is understood.

Second, the bolded phrases indicate the use of Spanish word order and inflection. The use of "qualyty final" instead of "final quality" reflects Spanish word order whereby adjectives follow nouns. The use of "operationals incidents" reflects Spanish inflection rules requiring adjectives to agree with their nouns in number.

Finally, the italicized words indicate where the writer lacks an understanding of U.S. idioms. He uses "asking" for "answering"; instead of writing "Thank you for" or "Thanks to you," he writes "Thanks you"; and he attempts an idiom ("just *and* time" instead of "just in time").

Caveat: Between the Extremes

Between the two ends of the continuum are immigrant students whose families have chosen to come to the United States and whose education in their first language has been substantial, or whose first language may not have a written language, or who may have studied English as a foreign language before they arrived in the United States; or their situation may be any combination of these. Also along the continuum are international students who have come to the United States to study because they have not been successful in their own educational systems or whose study of both their first language and English has been limited.

There are also differences within the differences: parental attitudes toward education that include the belief that women should not attend college; a prior education system that values rote memorization or teacher-centered classrooms in which students do not participate orally; a culture that values reflective thought or cooperation above the analysis, confrontation, and competition valued in many U.S. classrooms. Finally, there are individual student differences in personality, learning styles, learning strategies, and motivation.

Initial Identification

For the teacher of a student who has second-language writing problems, discovering whether that student is a U.S. resident (language minority) student or an international student is the first step in identifying the student's problems and recommending resources for remediation. The process is simple: ask the student for background information so that appropriate resources and support can be recommended. Sample questions that might be asked include the following:

- Is English your second (or third or fourth) language?
- What is your first language?
- Did you graduate from a U.S. high school?

If the answer to the last question is no, the student is most likely an international student. If the answer is yes, the student is probably a U.S. resident (language minority) student.

Answers to such questions will differ according to students' prior experiences. For example, students who are U.S. residents may have studied several years in U.S. public schools and have had constant language support through an excellent ESL program. Such a student will probably have the necessary skills to succeed in college or university work with minimal external support. In contrast, the writing of a student who has attended only the last year or two in a U.S. high school, along with some classroom study of English prior to her arrival, may have a combination of international and resident errors that make solutions to writing problems more complex.

Acquiring written English will be easier for resident English-as-a-second-language writers who are fluent and literate in their first languages than for students who are semiliterate or illiterate in their first language. Furthermore, a student whose education has been interrupted (by war, flight, refugee camps, and the like) may also be older and may have problems outside of language learning. Finally, students who have attended U.S. schools for a significant period of time but whose formal ESL education has been spotty are often doubly disadvantaged. Orally fluent, they have developed (perhaps unconsciously) language "rules," some of which must be identified, unlearned, and relearned if they are to become successful academic writers. In the meantime, their prior experiences saddle them with failure, and both their reading and writing skills may be limited.

In contrast, international students can provide the teacher with actual data that will help analyze their writing problems. Most international students will have taken the TOEFL (Test of English as a Foreign Language), an examination that is required for admission at most U.S. colleges and universities. At present the test is a multiple choice examination used by most college and university admissions offices. It is designed and administered worldwide each month by the Educational Testing Service (ETS), the same educational corporation that administers the SAT, GMAT, and LSAT.

TOEFL scores can be quite revealing. An overall TOEFL score of 550 or above often indicates that the student is ready for full-time postsecondary work; a score below 500 usually indicates that the student should be taking intensive English language courses. The three section scores on the TOEFL indicate general proficiency in listening, grammar, and reading skills; those scores are reported in double digits, but adding a zero to a section score allows you to compare it with the overall TOEFL score. For example, a section score of 55 indicates that a student has adequate language proficiency for admission.

Students from different language backgrounds may have similar overall TOEFL scores, but their section scores may differ, indicating potential problems in U.S. classes. For instance, Asian students will often score well on grammar and reading (for example, 58), but less well on listening skills (45). These students may be able to keep up with university reading assignments, but they may have problems understanding lectures or working with other students. In contrast, Arabic students may score higher on the listening section and lower in the reading section; these students may seem fluent during class discussions, but they may have substantial problems completing reading assignments.

Several times a year, the Test of Written English (TWE) is added to the TOEFL exam; the TWE is a direct test of student writing and is evaluated holistically by ESL teachers at large scoring sessions held in California. The maximum score is 6; a score of 4.5 or better usually means that the student can do postsecondary written work. Scores lower than 4.0 suggest that those students may need focused work in U.S. academic writing. Unfortunately, many international students will not have a TWE score, either because it was not offered when they took the TOEFL examination or because they chose not to take it.

And many postsecondary institutions still have not accepted the TWE as a viable admissions tool. (For more information about the TOEFL and the TWE, ask the admissions office at your college or university, or write to the TOEFL Program, Educational Testing Service, Princeton, NJ 08541.)

Another variable in an international student's previous schooling may be attendance in an intensive English language program, either prior to their arrival in the United States or in a U.S. program. If students have studied ESL in the United States, they may have encountered the rhetoric of academic English writing and so may be relatively proficient in presenting written ideas; the concepts of topic sentence, supporting detail, and essay structure may be familiar to them. Even the students who have studied English intensively prior to their arrival may not have encountered formal and stylistic principles of academic writing (Leki, 1992).

Error Gravity

Before teachers approach English-as-a-second-language student writing, they should know about "error gravity," that is, understand that some grammatical and syntactic errors are more serious than others (see Holt's chapter). Errors that interfere with comprehension are more substantial than those that do not. For example, errors in word order, verb tense, and word choice prevent the reader from making sense of the message. Of these, word order is often the most serious error, yet for students from some language backgrounds, word order in English is particularly difficult. The English sentence that follows has been translated into correct Korean and then back-translated directly, word for word, into English. The problem of word order is evident:

> *English:* Even though I told John not to take the chemistry class, he took it.
> *Korean:* Even though I John chemistry class not to take told John it took.

The following are less serious errors because they do not usually interfere with the direct communication of ideas: article mistakes, incorrect preposition choice, lack of pronoun agreement, comma splices, and spelling mistakes. However, some readers who are native English speakers may be irritated by these errors and may consider the student who produces them a poor writer. Thus these "less serious" errors become major ones. Article and preposition errors, for instance, are the most difficult for many English-as-a-second-language writers to remediate for several possible reasons: (1) articles do not occur in their first language; (2) English article rules are very complex; (3) prepositions do not occur, or do not occur in such numbers, in their first language; and (4) preposition rules in English are particularly arbitrary.

To summarize:

• English-as-a-second-language errors must be seen in the context of communicative purpose.

- They need to be prioritized if English-as-a-second-language writers are to benefit from remediation.
- Some errors are almost never 100 percent remediable. Fortunately, these errors do not usually interfere with reader comprehension.
- For such errors (in particular, articles and prepositions), English-as-a-second-language writers should spend their time more wisely on other, more serious errors, and ask a native English speaker for assistance in correcting the articles and prepositions in their writing.

Remediation

By identifying student writing errors and then by asking the student writers about their errors, the teacher can better suggest resources for student assistance. Phrase the questions in ways that will elicit information about the student's knowledge, without accusation, as demonstrated by the following examples:

Don't Say:	*Try Saying:*
"This is wrong."	"Do you see the error here?"
"Fix this."	"How might you fix this?"
"Why did you write this?"	"Do you know about . . . ?"
"You made a mistake here."	"Did you learn about . . . ?"

If the level of trust is high—that is, if the student is sure that the conference is being held to help not to judge him, he will be more able to identify what he doesn't know (or what he "knows" incorrectly) and more accepting of the suggestions for remediation and assistance.

Once the teacher has determined whether student writers are U.S. residents (language minority) or international students, there are many resources for remediation on college or university campuses. The teacher may therefore direct students to qualified personnel for writing assistance. For example, if students are U.S. residents, they have direct access to federally funded student programs on the campus for help and tutoring (and perhaps test accommodation) in writing, reading, and math. The students (or the teacher) can contact those offices for short- and long-term assistance, and the teacher can require that the students seek this assistance. Often the support offered by these offices provides the necessary scaffolding and encouragement that resident students need to achieve successful learning experiences.

Generally speaking, international students are not eligible for such federal assistance, although some colleges and universities do not discriminate (or simply do not know the difference). International students who have had prior experience with an intensive English language program on or near the campus have access to previous teachers in that program; those teachers have knowledge of other campus options. In addition, because of their prior English language study, international students are usually capable of using a handbook or a dictionary to check their errors and to expand their knowledge of English grammar and mechanics. However, because handbooks for native speakers of English do not address English-as-a-second-language problems effectively, I suggest one of the following:

- Ascher, A. *Think About Editing: A Grammar Editing Guide for ESL Writers.* Boston: Heinle and Heinle, 1993.
- Byrd, P., and Benson, B. *Improving the Grammar of Written English: The Handbook.* Belmont, Calif.: Wadsworth Publishing, 1989.
- Byrd, P., and Benson, B. *Improving the Grammar of Written English: The Editing Process.* Belmont, Calif.: Wadsworth Publishing, 1989.
- Byrd, P., and Benson, B. *Problem/Solution: A Reference for ESL Writers.* Boston: Heinle and Heinle, 1994.
- *Dictionary of American English.* Boston: Heinle and Heinle, 1996.
- Lange, J., and Lange, E. *Writing Clearly: An Editing Guide.* Boston: Heinle and Heinle, 1993.

Another campus resource that is available to all English-as-a-second-language student writers is the campus writing center (or writing laboratory). The writing center should be seen by teachers and English-as-a-second-language students as a valuable resource that will support English-as-a-second-language writers throughout their postsecondary careers. Moreover, paid tutors, often accessible through the international student services/education office, the intensive English language program, or the English department, can provide necessary support for English-as-a-second-language writers.

Native English-speaking friends can also serve as editors and language informants. I advise my ESL students about appropriate approaches to such assistance:

- Do not expect a friend to write, revise, or rewrite your paper.
- Sit with your native English-speaking friend and learn from her: identify specific problems, ask specific questions, and draw conclusions and learn!
- Ask politely for assistance; don't demand.
- Offer a friendly trade by providing pizza for proofing or by exchanging language and cultural information.
- Say thanks, with a smile.

Finally, for the many resident and international student writers whose rhetorical background is limited, the resources cited in the list that follows can help. First-year composition textbooks for native English-speaking writers may not address the differences that distinguish the rhetoric of academic prose in the United States from the rhetorics with which non-native students are familiar in their own cultures. However, there are materials written for English-as-a-second-language writers that explain U.S. academic rhetoric and provide adequate practice for the students. Among those texts are the following:

- Leki, I. *Academic Writing: Exploring Processes and Strategies.* (2nd ed.) New York: St. Martin's Press, 1995.
- Mlynarczyk, R., and Haber, S. *In Our Own Words: A Guide with Readings for Student Writers.* New York: St. Martin's Press, 1996.
- Reid, J. *The Process of Composition.* (2nd ed.) Englewood Cliffs, N.J.: Prentice Hall/Regents, 1988.
- Spack, R. *Guidelines: A Cross-Cultural Reading/Writing Text.* (2nd ed.) New York: St. Martin's Press, 1996.
- Weissberg, R., and Buker, S. *Writing up Research: Experimental Research Report Writing for Students of English.* Englewood Cliffs, N.J.: Prentice Hall/Regents, 1990.

Conclusion

The word *remediation* in this chapter is not meant to suggest that English-as-a-second-language student writers are any less cognitively capable than other postsecondary students. Indeed, learning and using a second language, attending and participating in classes in another language, and writing for an audience with different linguistic, rhetorical, and cultural expectations are extremely challenging tasks. English-as-a-second-language students need information and practice in specific areas of academic prose such as content and organization. Many U.S. residents (language minority) have only limited (and sometimes incorrect) ideas about English grammar and written communication. Therefore, for both of these groups, their growth and experience in academic writing should not include banishment to workbook exercises or denigration by teachers who are irritated by missing articles. Moreover, all English-as-a-second-language writers—both immigrant and international students—need additional linguistic and rhetorical information, careful analysis of their writing weaknesses by professionals in the field of teaching ESL, and consistent support and resources to improve their skills.

Finally, teachers and students must expect that improvement in English-as-a-second-language writing will be neither quick nor easy. Writing in a second language involves an even more complex set of cognitive tasks than writing as a native speaker. Grammar "rules" that have been habituated must be unlearned; rhetorical expectations of a lifetime must be changed, at least for the time the student presents ideas in written English; audience expectations (cultural, rhetorical, contextual, and linguistic) must be identified and fulfilled. Time, effort, understanding, energy, patience, trust—without these qualities, both teachers and English-as-a-second-language student writers will be frustrated.

Reference

Leki, I. *Understanding ESL Writers: A Guide for Teachers.* New York: St. Martin's Press, 1992.

JOY M. REID is an associate professor in the Department of English at the University of Wyoming. Her publications include Teaching ESL Writing *and an edited volume,* Learning Styles in the ESL/EFL Classroom.

This chapter looks at the influence students' native languages have on their comprehension of the Anglo-Saxon and Greco-Latinate elements of English vocabulary. It ends with suggestions for teachers and learners.

Why Do They Get It When I Say "Gingivitis" But Not When I Say "Gum Swelling"?

Bruce Maylath

Maybe you have experienced a scenario like this one. You are teaching a class on anatomy, focusing this day on the teeth, jaw, and mouth, and somehow a question comes up about tooth decay and its consequences. "I'd better mention gingivitis," you think to yourself, but then you realize that the majority of students in your class have probably never heard the word before. So, quite naturally, you decide instead to use a phrase you are sure they do know, "a swelling of the gum."

Unfortunately, as you continue to talk about teeth eventually falling out if the gum swells for a long enough period, you notice a student from Brazil staring at you with a fearful look in his eye, and you note that his mouth, which for the past hour had been chomping on chewing gum, has slowed to a stop in mid-chew. At about this point you mention that the technical term for gum swelling is "gingivitis." The Brazilian suddenly laughs and begins chewing again. Curious, you say to him, "You look relieved, Paulo. What's going on?" Paulo responds, "Before you said 'gingivitis,' I thought you were saying that chewing gum could make your teeth swell and fall out. Now I see that the place that holds your teeth is called 'gum,' too."

How is it that Paulo knew a complex word like *gingivitis* but not a simple, little word like *gum* of the tooth-holding kind? It so happens that the word for gum in Paulo's language is *gingivo,* and the word for gum swelling sounds very much like "gingivitis." As a Brazilian, Paulo speaks Portuguese, a successor language to Latin. Its siblings in the Romance language family include Catalan, French, Italian, Romanian, and Spanish. It turns out that Paulo is often much more comfortable with biology terminology in English than his native English-speaking classmates are.

Which Words Are the Hard Words?

This scenario yields several points important for teachers in all fields. First, the words that native English speakers find difficult may not be particularly hard for students with other home languages, especially if those home languages are among the Romance languages. Second, some words, like *gum,* which native English speakers think of as simple or easy, may not be so simple to define or easy to learn for international students. Many such words have multiple, unrelated meanings or appear in idioms. Third, if you are a native English speaker, the teaching strategies that you take for granted when you help native English speakers learn the specialized vocabulary of your discipline may confuse international students.

Why is this the case? And what can you do to help both groups? The rest of this chapter supplies some answers.

Where English Words Come From

Although scientific terms in English are in one sense English, in another sense they are still foreign. Typically they are made up of Latin or Greek elements. In English-speaking countries, subject areas such as biology, chemistry, physics, psychology, and sociology devote much of their time to teaching the specialized vocabulary of the discipline, almost all of whose words come from Latin or Greek. For example, a sampling of common anatomical terms breaks down this way:

Germanic	*Latinate*
belly	abdomen
jaw	mandible
skull	cranium
teeth	dentition

Although the terms in the right-hand column stem from Latin, English borrowed many of its scientific words from Greek as well. Latin, however, also provided English with many nonscientific words through the Romance languages. Indeed, the vocabulary of English is largely an uneasy marriage of words from two distinct language families: the Germanic and the Romance. Most of the Germanic words are Anglo-Saxon, with a number added from Old Norse during the Viking invasions of the British Isles. Many of the Romance words came to English from French, when William the Conqueror and his soldiers from Normandy invaded England in 1066. Many more came directly from Latin during the Renaissance, when lawyers, scholars, priests, and scribes wanted to write in English but used words to which they had grown accustomed when they wrote in Latin. As a result, many an Anglo-Saxon word comes with a French or Latin synonym or one-time equivalent:

Germanic	Romance
to understand	to comprehend
to better	to improve
to put or set	to place
swine	pork
sheep	mutton
house	mansion
strength	forte
freedom	liberty
last	final
hindsight	retrospect
cunning	savvy

Because the words come from different languages, they often have different shades of meaning. *Waterproof* and *impermeable,* for example, are Germanic and Romance equivalents, but *impermeable* is somewhat more flexible and can be applied to any barrier.

Why Different Students Have Trouble with Different Words

People have little trouble making sense of so-called big words if they can pull them apart into little words. *Waterproof,* for instance, is obviously two words put together. If you know what *water* and *proof* (as in "barrier") mean by themselves, you can readily understand what *waterproof* means when the two parts are combined to make a larger word. Linguists and language psychologists call such words "transparent." Nearly all languages combine elements in this way more or less, taking everyday words for concrete ideas and combining them to form bigger words representing abstract ideas. Thus, if you ask five-year-olds what they think might happen in an "afterlife," they can be surprisingly conversant, even though the concept of an afterlife has to be one of the most abstract ideas to exist in any language. Understanding, remembering, and using a word for an abstract idea is not hard if you can pull the word apart into pieces you already use and understand: in this case, *after* and *life.* (By the way, if you did not already know, those compound words like *waterproof* and *afterlife* are Anglo-Saxon, or Old English. They are not borrowed, nor are their parts. They belong to the Germanic language family, rather than the Romance.)

If most languages form words in this way, what then is the problem with English? In a word, opacity. It is difficult for English speakers to hear or view a word from the Romance family and know at a glance what it means. Romance words' opacity is the result of the English language's strange history and its native English speakers' habits. For more than nine hundred years, English speakers have tended to borrow words from other languages, particularly French after the Norman Conquest and Latin and Greek from the Renaissance on. Unfortunately, these borrowed words are hard for English speakers to pull apart and make sense of—English speakers simply do not use the parts of these words by themselves. Thus, if we take the earlier example, *waterproof,* and look at its Latinate equivalent in English, *impermeable,* we have a much harder time seeing its meaning at a glance. The only part that we would be quick to use by itself is *able.* The stem, *perme-,* turns out to be especially troublesome. Its meaning, "pass through" or "go through," remains opaque to most English speakers, unless they have learned Latin or, like Paulo, have grown up speaking a Romance language. *Impermeable,* then, means literally "not-through-go-able," or "not able to go through" when rendered in idiomatic English. Notably, *impermeable* is pretty common in Paulo's language. Not only is it related to the word for waterproof, it is also related to the word for raincoat.

Although English draws its vocabulary from both the Germanic and Romance language families, when adults speak with children, they use the Germanic words almost exclusively, something David Corson (1985, 1995) discovered when he examined the vocabularies of schoolchildren in England and Australia. Moreover, books in English aimed at children under twelve are written overwhelmingly in a Germanic vocabulary. This is not because young children cannot understand Romance words like *impermeable:* children from Buenos Aires to Montreal to Naples and Bucharest use such words—and often only such words—every day. However, because of the complicated history of word borrowing in English, English-speaking adults assume that their children cannot and should not learn words borrowed from French, Latin, or Greek until around age fifteen. As a result, these children often do not learn the big words until high school and may avoid them even then, a phenomenon Corson calls "lexical avoidance." Avoidance of Greek and Latinate words, especially for the working classes, is reinforced by peer and family pressure, resulting in what Corson terms "lexical apartheid" from the professional classes. In other words, the native English speakers in your classroom may have trouble learning words like *gingivitis* in part because such words are opaque in meaning, and in part because the students have lacked exposure to such words and may have even willfully avoided them.

What about the international students? Their obstacles to learning English vocabulary are much more varied. Paulo's confusion is just one example of what can happen when international students encounter English words. Clearly, students with Romance-language backgrounds will usually have an easier time learning the specialized Greek and Latinate terms across the curriculum than will those without. In fact, Corson (1985) found that working-class Australian students who spoke Italian, Spanish, or Portuguese at home outscored working-class Australian students who spoke English at home when both groups took tests. He attributed this phenomenon to the first group's greater ease with the Greek and Latinate vocabulary used on many secondary school tests, especially science tests.

On the other hand, students from countries where Germanic languages are spoken—Austria, Denmark, the Netherlands, Norway, Sweden, Germany, and parts of Belgium and Switzerland—will often face the same problems of opacity when they encounter Romance words that native English speakers face. Unless they have studied Latin or a living Romance language thoroughly, *impermeable* will seem just as big, dense, and opaque to them. *Waterproof,* on the other hand, will look familiar and will operate like the compounds in their own languages when pulled apart. For example, the word *waterproof* is *water-dicht* in Dutch, *wasserdicht* in German, and *vanntett* in Norwegian. *Dicht* and *tett* are cognates of the English *tight;* the speakers of those languages are literally saying "watertight."

However, most of your international students may come from the Far East, the Middle East, the Near East, or Africa—or perhaps their families did. For these students virtually *all* English words seem opaque. There will be a few exceptions. A significant number of English words, whether Anglo-Saxon or Greek and Latinate, have made their way into other languages. Japanese, for example, has borrowed the word *baseball,* which they pronounce "be-su ba-ru." Also, English has borrowed words from some of their languages: *bungalow,* for instance, comes from Hindi. Quite a few words from Latin and Greek, especially scientific terms, have made their own separate way into many languages, English included. Hence, the Greek word *hydrogen* is known by virtually the same name (*hydrogène*) in French, even though in Norwegian, a sibling language of English, it's called *vannstoff* (literally "waterstuff"—the building material of water). Thus, your students at home with African or Asian languages (and these include Finnish and Hungarian) are not likely to have an easy time with any English words, although they may find a smattering of Greek and Latinate technical terms more familiar than the Anglo-Saxon words you have thought of as uncomplicated and relatively commonplace.

Multiple Meanings

Here is something else to keep in mind about Anglo-Saxon words. Although their meanings often seem more transparent than Greek and Latinate words, especially when it comes to compounds, Anglo-Saxon words often take on more than one meaning in English—meanings that may seem unrelated. Consider Paulo's confusion with *gum.* He had had lots of contact with the variety with which he could blow bubbles, but he had not had any reason before this to learn about the variety that holds the teeth in place. Because both varieties are found in the mouth and the class lecture involved the mouth, he assumed the word he had heard matched the meaning he already knew.

What Paulo did not know—and what most English speakers do not know either—is that the two meanings of *gum* come from different sources: as commonly happens in such cases, one comes from a Germanic language and one from a Romance. The one that you the instructor meant, "firm flesh around roots of teeth," as the *Concise Oxford Dictionary* defines it, is Anglo-Saxon and was spelled *goma* in Old English. The one that Paulo already knew—the kind he was chewing—is actually a French import dating back to the Norman Conquest. In Old French it was spelled *gomme*. When Anglo-Saxon and Norman French collided in 1066, words that sounded somewhat similar often grew nearer and nearer in pronunciation. As a result, many words eventually ended up with identical spellings, even though their multiple meanings could differ wildly. Another example is *seal*. How is it that the word refers both to a "fish-eating amphibious marine mammal of the family Phocidae or Otariidae" and to a piece of wax, metal, or adhesive that has been impressed? As you might suspect, the name for the mammal comes from Anglo-Saxon (*seolh* in Old English), whereas the name for the impression made its way in with the Normans. Spelled *seel* in Old French, it is itself a contracted form of Latin *sigillum*, a diminutive for *signum*, from which English later took its words *sign, signify*, and *signature*. You may find that your international students know the Old French meaning, as they've frequently used envelopes, but they may never have had occasion to learn the Anglo-Saxon meaning.

Idioms

Idioms are phrases that mean something different from what they appear to mean on the surface. Every language uses idioms, and English is no different in this regard. For instance, Paulo is trying to identify a tissue in one of your labs and tells you, "This is difficult," to which you reply, "Nonsense. It's a piece of cake." Hearing that, Paulo is likely to cast you another of his jaw-frozen stares of confusion. Clearly, your words carry a different meaning from the one Paulo sees on the surface.

Idioms are not simply slang. Slang includes words and meanings that are not considered formal, such as when your North American students say "Cool" or, in more recent years, "Sweet!" to mean they are pleased. Certainly some idioms meet this definition, but by no means do all. Many idioms are used in even the most formal writing: "to make a clean breast of something" is more likely to be used in formal settings than in informal. Of course, if we wanted to translate it from Germanic to Romance, we would say "to confess." In informal settings we might make this verb sound Germanic by changing it to "'fess up." All of these idiomatic phrases mean something different from what a non-native speaker would guess just going by the words' other meanings or by looking them up individually in a dictionary.

Hyperfluency

Both native and non-native English speakers may find reasons to adopt Greek and Latinate words in their writing. First, they are likely to want to show that they have learned the vocabulary introduced in your course. As mentioned earlier, the bulk of this specialized terminology is probably Greek and Latin. Second, they may "overchoose." (Yes, I've coined a new term in "overchoose" by combining transparent, everyday Germanic words.) They will overchoose Greek and Latinate words merely for prestige reasons, throwing in such terms willy-nilly, sometimes using words in ways you have never seen before. Balester (1991) identifies this phenomenon as "hyperfluency." At times it may seem that students have opened a thesaurus and substituted every Greek and Latinate synonym they could for an Anglo-Saxon word, just to impress you with their word knowledge. If your international students have been around awhile, you may find them doing the same, particularly if they come from a rigidly hierarchical society with British influence, such as India or Sri Lanka.

Unfortunately, your students may be getting reinforcement for loading on the Romance vocabulary in their composition courses, especially if they are taught by a new teaching assistant. A teaching assistant with less than two years' experience at teaching writing appears to be much more likely than those with more experience to favor writing fraught with Greco-Latinate terms (Maylath, 1996). Because nearly all composition courses at large U.S. universities are taught by such teachers, the majority of whom are new to teaching, the undergraduates at these institutions may be getting a large dose of reinforcement for turning to the thesaurus at every opportunity. If you teach at such an institution, you'll need to tell your students explicitly which Greek and Latinate terms are appropriate, which are not, and why.

Steps You and Your Students Can Take

In addition to talking to your class about your own views on word choice, you can direct your proficient international students to several avenues that will help them make sense of English words. First, advise them to use a good desk dictionary with etymologies. Then show them how to use the etymologies to see the lexical patterns and stem meanings, as explained earlier. My favorite is the *Concise Oxford Dictionary,* as it is based on the unabridged *Oxford English Dictionary,* upon which many other dictionaries base their etymologies. Similarly, the *Oxford American Dictionary* comes from the same publisher and focuses, as the name suggests, on American entries. Many good versions of the *Merriam Webster Dictionary* and the *American Heritage Dictionary* also include etymologies. Perhaps the best advice is to warn students that pocket dictionaries usually omit etymologies, something about which they will not be concerned unless you demonstrate that you value such information.

Second, tell your international students to find a dictionary of English idioms. My favorite is *English Idioms and How to Use Them* (Seidl and McMordie, 1978), a surprisingly comprehensive pocket guide.

Third, some international students benefit greatly from working with native English speakers in small groups. (See Nelson's and Johnson's chapters on peer response groups.) This is often the best way for them to learn idioms and Anglo-Saxon words—from natives, in context. It is not a bad way to learn Greek and Latinate words either. Unfortunately, international students are often isolated from much spoken contact with native English speakers, whether in their living quarters, in classrooms, or in social settings. This is partly because of differences in language and culture, but also because of the way university classes, particularly large ones, are conducted. Although classrooms are the one place where international students regularly find themselves seated next to native English speakers, and thus would seem to have an opportunity to learn English from interaction, the lecture system tends to obliterate these opportunities. Even five minutes devoted to small-group discussions of an idea presented in the course can lead to tremendous gains in an international student's acquisition of vocabulary and fluency. Having made initial contact in class, international students are more likely to continue conversations with the native students outside of class, and so gain far more language practice.

Fourth, several books on language roots may help clarify for your international students what I have explained above. Volume two of the series *Origins: The Word Families* by Robinson with McAuliffe (1989) does an especially good job of showing relationships among Anglo-Saxon words as well as Greek and Latinate words. Although written for young American students, the book's accessibility will prove helpful to international students as well.

Fifth, some universities offer classes in Greek and Latin etymology for pre-medicine majors or nurses. Highly tailored, these courses can benefit international as well as native English speakers in the specialized Greek and Latinate vocabulary they will encounter in the health sciences.

Finally, you, the instructor, can help international students immediately by identifying their home languages and watching for signs of misunderstanding or confusion. Once you are aware that the words and idioms that seem simple and easy to native English speakers are often not so simple and easy to non-native speakers, you may decide that it makes sense to express an idea in more than one way. You can use redundancy to your students' advantage, and you'll have good precedent. The English lexicon, particularly the law, is filled with seemingly redundant pairs of words drawn one each from Germanic and Romance sources. "Last will and testament" is one of the most common; others include "breaking and entering," "deem and consider," and "shun and avoid" (Mellinkoff, 1963). This redundancy in communication is not merely a vestige of England's age of Norman rule. As recently as 1892, A. E. Housman is reported to have delivered his "Introductory Lecture" at University College, London, by repeating each point twice, once in Latinate English, once in Germanic, in an attempt to reach all segments of his audience (Lanham, 1983). In one sense, those of us who lecture today do the same, but we think of our technique as explaining an idea in formal, academic language, then in everyday English. Often, doing so helps not only the non-native speakers but the native speakers, too.

References

Balester, V. M. "Hyperfluency and the Growth of Linguistic Resources." *Language and Education,* 1991, *5,* 81–94.

Corson, D. *The Lexical Bar*. New York: Pergamon Press, 1985.

Corson, D. *Using English Words*. Dordrecht, the Netherlands: Kluwer, 1995.

Lanham, R. *Analyzing Prose*. Old Tappan, N.J.: Macmillan, 1983.

Maylath, B. "Words Make a Difference: The Effects of Greco-Latinate and Anglo-Saxon Lexical Variation on College Writing Instructors." *Research in the Teaching of English,* 1996, *30* (2), 220–247.

Mellinkoff, D. *The Language of the Law*. New York: Little, Brown, 1963.

Robinson, S. R., with McAuliffe, L. *Origins: The Word Families*. Vol. 2. New York: Teachers and Writers Collaborative, 1989.

Seidl, J., and McMordie, W. *English Idioms and How to Use Them*. Oxford: Oxford University Press, 1978.

BRUCE MAYLATH is an assistant professor of English in the Department of English at the University of Memphis. He teaches in the Professional and Technical Writing program. He has taught ESL in Michigan and English as a Foreign Language in Norway.

Because Muslim students are a significant part of many college campuses, professors need to know how to work with these students in the classroom. Through interviews, Muslim students provide examples of problems they have encountered in the American classroom, and solutions to those problems.

Respect for Religious Differences: The Case of Muslim Students

Bruce W. Speck

"On the outside, professors want to look like they are open . . . ready to accept any idea." That is the observation of a Muslim student—I will call him Abu—who has lived in the United States fifteen years. Abu went on to remark that the professors' attitudes are merely "camouflage." Abu felt that when confronted with Islamic practice—including fasting, prayer five times daily, acceptance of polygamy, and strict punishment for crimes—many professors are in reality anything but tolerant.

Professors may have two responses to Abu's remarks. Some may say, "My job is to teach my subject area in a climate comfortable for my students. I have no interest in learning about Islam." To those professors, I suggest that to create a climate comfortable for students requires some understanding of what presuppositions students bring to the classroom. In the case of international students who have learned English as a second language, we can easily lose sight of what it means to be both a cultural stranger and a member of a minority religion. We can exhibit biases that interfere with the teaching-learning process for some of our students, as Abu reminds us. Throw in, in some cases, international students' linguistic inability to defend themselves, and the problem can become disabling.

Professors might have a second response, however. Professors who see that Abu's position might be viable may well ask, "Do most Muslims feel this way? Or is Abu's position idiosyncratic?" I have found little research to answer those questions.

To explore reasons for possible religious bias among professors, I initiated a two-part research project, which I restricted to Muslim students because (1) Islam is one of the fastest-growing religions in the world, and (2) Muslim students are generally a significant part of the international student population on university campuses. For Part One of the study, a Muslim graduate student distributed a questionnaire to Muslim students at a Friday prayer time. Muslim students' responses indicate encounters with religious prejudice, but those who completed questionnaires gave few examples of such prejudice (Speck, 1996). As a follow-up, in Part Two I interviewed four Muslim students individually. The Muslim graduate student who had assisted me in Part One selected interviewees from the students who had indicated on the questionnaire that Muslim students will encounter religious prejudice and who were willing to relate specific examples of such prejudice.

An analysis of the transcribed interviews revealed that students identified the following four problems: (1) professors' misunderstanding of Muslim practices may result in misrepresenting them in the classroom; (2) professors may use media that introduce misunderstandings about Islam; (3) professors may fail to maintain attitudes of respect for certain religions in the classroom; and (4) professors may not make an effort to accommodate students' religious practices. What follows is based on the problems students identified and the solutions they offered. For ease of reading, I have given pseudonyms to each interviewee: Hassan (undergraduate male), Fatima (undergraduate female), Abu (male graduate student), Haleema (female graduate student).

Problem One: Misrepresenting Muslim Students in the Classroom

The consensus of the interviewees was that most professors do not adequately understand the variety of practice in Islam. As Haleema noted, professors "associate Saudi Arabia with Muslims all over the world," but the practices in Saudi Arabia are not representative of Muslim practices worldwide. Fatima also pointed out that "there is no Islamic culture per se because different countries incorporate their culture into their religion." For instance, "Women don't drive in Saudi Arabia, but it's not religious doctrine. It's just the culture of Saudi Arabia."

Beyond general misperceptions about Islam, interviewees noted that Americans as a group do not understand Islamic practices such as polygamy, covering (particularly the wearing of a *hijab,* the head covering, by Muslim women), modesty of dress in general, and fasting, particularly fasting associated with Ramadan. For instance, Haleema gave an example of a professor who discussed polygamy in Islam. Although Haleema did not report the professor's words, her observation of the presentation was, "He may have understood it, but the way he represented it to students—I just thought he could have done a better job," implying that his presentation did not clearly represent polygamy in Islam. However, students may find it difficult to correct misperceptions, in part because, as Haleema said, students believe the professor is "an authority. They're going to believe him." Another problem may be language limitations.

Thus, international students who are Muslims may not feel they have an adequate command of the language to raise objections to a professor.

In offering students' solutions to any of the problems they cite, I recognize that international students may come from cultures where the classroom setting is informed by a different set of rules than the classroom setting in the United States. For instance, students in some cultures simply do not question the professor's views. In addition, in a culture with a commitment to a particular religion, like Islam, Muslim students are not faced with the problems of pluralism that are part and parcel of the American university classroom. Thus, solutions to problems concerning religious bias in the university classroom can be complicated by the perspectives of students from other cultures. With that in mind, consider the following solutions to the misrepresentation of religion in the classroom.

1. *Recognize your preconceptions.* Perhaps the best way to approach the problem of recognizing our preconceptions is to consider the interviewees' examples of what appear to be unconscious presuppositions resulting in prejudicial actions. For instance, Fatima has come to recognize that her dress can be confused with her lack of mastery of English. She said, "Because I wear the *hijab,* I think [professors] don't like to talk to me as much because they think I don't speak English. That kind of attitude is irritating. And if I do speak English, they are just so grateful, like, 'O God, she speaks English.'" Fatima's remarks are particularly striking to me because during our interview, her spoken English was excellent.

Abu offered another example. He was engaged in a discussion with his science professor in which he and the professor were batting around ideas about how to approach a particular research problem. Abu recounts the conversation as follows:

PROFESSOR (seemingly in response to the scientific discussion he had been having with Abu): Well you know, somebody could think that they are 100 percent right and they could be 100 percent wrong.
ABU: Yes, this is true, but that's the beauty of science. If you never check, you will never know if you are right or if you are wrong . . .
PROFESSOR: I wasn't talking about science. I was talking about religion.

After this, Abu discontinued the conversation, thinking the following: "Whatever I was saying, [he interpreted from the viewpoint that I] . . . was just a Muslim, and he was saying [I] didn't know much because I'm 100 percent wrong as far as my faith is concerned."

The interviewees do not explain how professors can deal with personal bias based on presuppositions, but perhaps a first step in dealing with personal bias is to recognize it. Such recognition is a beginning step in learning how to treat with civility people who hold religious perspectives at variance with our own. As Hairston says, "a teacher who believes in diversity must pay attention to and respect students with deep religious convictions, not force them . . . into silence" (1992, p. 191).

2. *Become culturally alert.* Haleema stated the problem of professors' need for information about cultures in this way: "I don't feel American professors know much about other cultures. I think they need to learn about different cultures a lot." A variety of resources are available for professors to learn about religions. For instance, professors can visit Muslim student religious or cultural groups on campus and at local mosques. Professors also can read literature produced by organizations that represent Islam. Hassan cautioned, however, that not every organization that claims to represent Islam represents mainstream Islam. He recommended that professors contact the Islamic Society of North America (ISNA, P.O. Box 38, Plainfield, IN 46168) or the Islamic Circle of North America (ICNA, 166–26 89th Ave., Jamaica, NY 11432; tel. 718/658–1199) for materials on Islam. One scholarly journal that might interest professors is *The Muslim World.*

Although professors might agree that they need to learn about other cultures, they also might wonder when they will have time to do so. Is it realistic for professors to take Hassan seriously when he says, "I think it is the responsibility of each single instructor at this school to know the students [in his or her class]: what country they come from and their backgrounds"? Although Hassan does have a valid point, most of us cannot spend hours in the library learning about world religions. We can, however, select one religion, such as Islam, and become familiar with its religious practices and concepts. For instance, we can ask a Muslim student to have lunch with us and explain some of the major tenets of his or her religion. (In asking a Muslim student to lunch, we should find out about dietary restrictions the student might have.) We can watch videos about Islam. For example, Ambrose Video Publishing (28 West 44th St., Suite 2100, New York, NY 10036; tel. 1–800–526–4663) produces a set of six videos on Islam entitled *Living Islam: What It Means to Be a Muslim in Today's World.*

3. *Seek points of contact.* Abu suggested that people of different religious persuasions can live in greater harmony with each other if they recognize the commonality among religions. He said, "Once you teach someone the six articles of [the Muslim] faith, then a person of non-Islamic faith will realize actually that there's a lot of similarity between the religions, and if you try to work out or work toward the similarities and forgive each other or try to understand each other on our differences, then a bridge will be made. But if you keep the differences always then a wall will be made."

Problem Two: Professors' Media May Introduce Misunderstandings About Islam

As Hassan said, not every organization that purports to represent Islam faithfully represents Islam. This creates no small problem for professors. As outsiders, how do we know which sources are accurately portraying a particular religion?

Although the problem of legitimate sources is thorny, interviewees were quite emphatic about what sources are biased: U.S. news media and textbooks. All four interviewees criticized the U.S. news media for bias, but Haleema was quite pointed in her assessment: "The media just want to show one side of Islam. . . . Sometimes I think [the media] . . . are purposefully misleading." Shaheen (1988) agrees.

For example, Fatima talked about a class in which the teacher brought in an article on current events that reported how Algerian women who did not cover themselves were beaten by fanatics. The teacher's attitude, Fatima said, was that the fanatics' actions were normative. Fatima disagreed, saying in the interview, "That wasn't true. It's more like an isolated incident."

Abu provided another example. He recounted seeing a television program on a U.S. network around 1980 that celebrated Khadafi's industrial renovation of Libya. Abu was surprised at the positive image U.S. television portrayed of Khadafi, saying, "We always knew that Khadafi was nothing but a butcher." Abu went on to say that six or seven years later, U.S. television aired a counter report about how corrupt Khadafi was. That was just before President Reagan ordered the bombing of Libya. Abu's interpretation of the two programs about Khadafi was that U.S. television is not designed to give accurate news: "It's not to give by far the truth."

In addition to problems with bias in news media, interviewees noted that textbooks present distorted views of Islam. The consensus among interviewees was stated succinctly by Hassan, who said he found misperceptions about Islam in textbooks "most of the time." Fatima recounted a particular class in which "the book stated a case where Iranian women ate the leftovers of the men after the family dinner. The teacher just assumed that was what all Iranian women did, and there's just no way I would eat after anybody. The attitude [is] that women are slaves or second-class citizens. It was the cultural example [in the textbook], and maybe it happens in one case, but I know a lot of Iranian women, and they don't do that."

Abu discussed problems with what he perceived as a belittling of Islam in textbooks. For instance, he cited examples of textbooks that identify the Koran as "a book that is arranged or organized with the longest chapters in the beginning and the shorter chapters in the end." In commenting on this he said, "What a definition!" He gave a further example of how textbooks refer to Mohammed as "a man who came from Saudi Arabia and he claimed that he was given revelations from Allah. . . . Why do you say, 'he claimed'? If you say, 'he said,' then fine, but don't use the word *claim* because when you say 'claim' it means 'stated without proof.'"

The interviewees are saying that news media and textbooks cannot be trusted to interpret Islam accurately and that professors should not rely on news media and textbooks to learn about culture and religion. Rather, professors should check media reports and textbooks with other sources of information. According to Fatima, one way to check on the generalizability of media reports is to "talk with someone in Islam and see if [a particular news story is] a norm or if it's an isolated thing." She stressed the necessity of professors checking the generalizability of media reports because the media cover current events that could be discussed in class; when professors address those events they need to be aware of a variety of perspectives. Haleema claimed that professors "should have some more knowledge aside from information that they might have seen on TV. That's really not a reliable source to begin with for presenting information on any religion."

Professors also can call on Muslim students, or students from other religions, to give alternate points of view. When I asked Haleema about professors calling on Muslim students to give an opinion about Islam, she said, "Sure, I would think that would probably be the best thing. If not an expert, we would certainly have more knowledge than someone other than a Muslim."

Problem Three: Lack of Respect for Certain Religions in the Classroom

According to the interviewees, part of a professor's classroom responsibility is to intervene if students make insulting or misleading comments about religion. Hassan, however, gave an example of a professor's failure to intervene to correct students' misconception and ridicule of Islam. In one particular class, the students talked about covering, the custom in certain Iranian groups of women's wearing black veils. Hassan noted that the other students "started making fun of covering, and unfortunately the instructor did not stop them, although he knows that I'm a Muslim, and he knows the Middle East. He did not intervene or stop such comments."

Haleema alluded to the failure of a professor to intervene when she related an incident in which students ridiculed the penalty in an Islamic state of cutting off a person's hand for theft. According to Haleema, the students "were just really making fun, saying these people are so extreme and maybe we should try that. . . . People laugh, and what can you say? I mean it's true that is the penalty for theft but not like for a piece of candy or something really minor."

Students offered professors two solutions for maintaining respect for religion in the class.

1. *Intervene.* The students said that professors should not allow students in their classes to mock a particular religion or religious practice. As Haleema noted, cutting a person's hand off for stealing might be a means of stopping others from stealing. Although such a practice may seem extreme, other practices that are lawful in this country, such as capital punishment, also seem extreme to some people. In either case, the issue is debatable. So another way to intervene is to ask students to debate the issue or ask a student who holds to the particular practice to give a rationale to the class. The student might need time to prepare such a rationale. (Clearly, however, not all international students will be linguistically sophisticated enough to participate adequately in such a debate.)

2. *Apologize, if an apology is warranted.* Hassan related an incident in which he did approach a professor to clarify a point the professor had made about Islam. Hassan recounts, "I was so happy that the instructor said, although I don't want an instructor to say I'm sorry, but I really appreciate what he said. He said, 'I'm sorry if I ever offended you.' Some of the students came in and apologized for their comments."

Problem Four: Failure to Accommodate Students' Religious Practices

In affirming the importance of prayer, Abu discussed the conflict between offering prayers at specified times and attending lectures during those same times. "When lectures are scheduled on prayer time, then students are going to miss the lectures. I would say dedicated Muslims are going to miss them."

Haleema gave a different example of a professor who seemed to accommodate her practice of prayer but made a point of her leaving class when it came time for her to pray. Even though she had cleared the prayer time with the professor before the semester started, she recalled that "right when I was leaving . . . every class meeting he stopped and said, 'You are coming back, aren't you?' and of course I'm coming back. . . . And the funny part was he was teaching a section on Islam. . . . He knew the importance of prayer in Islam."

Abu also discussed the problem of Muslim students' attending departmental social functions when alcohol is served, saying, "by my faith I cannot go to a place where I know that there are intoxicants, any kind of intoxicant." Abu noted that other graduate students and faculty put pressure on him to participate in social events where alcohol was included and accused him of trying to prohibit alcohol from departmental social events. He tries to deal with this problem by attending the beginning of a social function and then leaving before alcohol is served.

According to interviewees, professors should try to accommodate religious practices, when possible. For instance, a professor should arrange for a Muslim student to leave class to pray. However, a prayer break may not be reasonable in the middle of an exam. At the beginning of the term, professors can invite students to discuss scheduling conflicts because of work, religious practices, or other obligations. Professors also can use a brief questionnaire at the beginning of the term to find out whether students need help to schedule times for their religious exercises, such as Muslim students who participate in Ramadan.

Conclusion

The four interviewees were clearly not promoting Islam for missionary purposes. Rather, they felt the need to promote a better understanding of Islam, in part to correct misconceptions that have led to prejudicial views of Islam. Hassan said as much: "We are asking for full, equal opportunity of knowledge. That's all what we ask for. . . . We are not asking someone, 'Come, oh come on—you want to convert to Islam?' Just learn about us."

Although I have suggested that the problems Muslims face may be generalizable to other religions, no empirical research that I know of supports that generalization. In fact, students from other religious persuasions might face similar or quite different problems. For instance, some Christians might object to the use of alcohol at departmental functions; some may not. However, researchers have shown that Christian students believe professors want them to leave their Christianity outside the classroom door (Ranieri and Dubinsky, 1995). We certainly are not required to be authorities on religion, but we do have an obligation to increase our knowledge about the social and religious viewpoints our students bring to our classes. We need to recognize the diversity in our classrooms and seek to ensure that whatever biases we have about religion or a religion do not become barriers to our responsibility to teach students.

References

Hairston, M. "Diversity, Ideology, and Teaching Writing." *College Composition and Communication,* 1992, *43,* 179–193.

Ranieri, P. W., and Dubinsky, J. "What Makes Collaboration Work: Cooperation, Care, and Respect." Paper presented at the annual meeting of the Association for General and Liberal Studies, San Antonio, Texas, Oct. 1995.

Shaheen, J. G. "The Media's Image of Arabs." *Newsweek,* Feb. 29, 1988, p. 10.

Speck, B. W. "Professor Bias, Religion, and ESL Students: The Need for a Reflective Pedagogy." *College Student Journal,* 1996, *30,* 390–397.

BRUCE W. SPECK *is an associate professor of English at the University of Memphis where he is coordinator of the writing-across-the-curriculum program.*

Students from different cultures follow differing norms for oral communication; this can affect the classroom and the students' grades. Patterns for differing norms are found in class discussions, question-and-answer sessions, small-group interactions, and formal class presentations.

Cultural Norms Affect Oral Communication in the Classroom

Ellen Johnson

Learning a language is more than just learning vocabulary, grammar, and sounds. A student also has to know the cultural rules that govern oral communication, such as acceptable amounts of talk, volume of speech, turn-taking processes, and pauses between speakers. Many international students and native English-speaking students from ethnic minorities may have expectations about the role of public speaking that differ from those of their instructors. Additionally, a paramount reason for learning about these cultural differences is to help teachers avoid underestimating students' intellectual abilities and learning levels in certain types of classroom interactions. Teachers need to understand both these rules and their students' perceptions to maximize all students' contributions.

Frequently, both teachers and students have difficulty in identifying communication problems, as it is hard to sort out the problem when the issue is the *way* something is said rather than *what* is said. In fact, teachers may not explicitly recognize and address differences in speaking patterns. However, misinterpretation can ensue because of differences in emphasis, politeness, and attitude, as indicated by tone, pitch, linking of words, and pauses (Bowers and Flinders, 1990, p. 87). This chapter helps professors recognize possible sources of miscommunication.

In discussing how professors can recognize such sources of miscommunication, I will focus on the following:

- Whole-class interaction: the teacher is interacting with the class as a whole—either through class discussion or during question-and-answer periods.
- Small-group interaction: the students are interacting with one another.

NEW DIRECTIONS FOR TEACHING AND LEARNING, no. 70, Summer 1997 © Jossey-Bass Publishers

• Student presentations: the students "perform" for the whole class in a formal way.

Students from different cultures will respond differently in these types of interactions. Therefore, teachers can vary their classroom procedures, but they cannot hope to conduct the class in a way that is always comfortable for all students all the time.

Whole-Class Interaction

It is easy to assume that when students refuse to respond to questions directed at the class, and especially to individuals, they do not answer because they do not know the information, have not done the required reading, or have no comprehension of important concepts. These may indeed be reasons for a lack of response, but there may be other reasons as well.

For instance, many cultures have a strong disdain for those who promote themselves as individuals rather than as part of the group. Students from such cultures may be reluctant to display their knowledge in front of the whole class. With Polynesians, for example, "the act of setting oneself above others, without some group-initiated and prior consent, infringes a complex cultural value" that is basic to their society (Corson, 1992, p. 474). In addition to a reluctance to display one's knowledge, there may be a sense of shame attached to making a mistake in public. Thus, many students will not volunteer a response in class, and they will hesitate to answer a question unless they are absolutely certain they are correct, even if they are called upon to respond.

Still other groups, including some Native Americans, are not accustomed to having to ask permission to speak, accomplished in the typical U.S. classroom by raising one's hand. Students who have been disciplined for speaking out without such permission may become reluctant to participate at all.

One problem with the question-and-answer scenario in the typical classroom is that of timing. Students from some Middle Eastern cultures may try to answer before the teacher even finishes the question. Such apparent interruptions are not only tolerated in their cultures but even encouraged as a sign of full engagement in the conversation. On the other hand, insufficient length of pauses is especially problematic for students whose native style of speaking includes longer spaces between turns. They may feel that questions are being fired at them without enough time to respond. For example, some Native American and Asian cultures place a high value on giving a reflective answer to a question, believing this style to be more courteous (Scarcella, 1990, p. 139). They see American students who respond quickly, sometimes by guessing, as impulsive and superficial. If students are nonresponsive, professors might try waiting longer before giving the answer themselves. In fact, this very act of the teacher's asking the class a question for which he or she already knows the answer may seem odd to some students (Scarcella, 1990, p. 137).

American university professors are often frustrated by what they see as a lack of classroom participation by foreign students. In our culture, fluency and talkativeness are seen as indicators of intelligence, competence, friendliness, and other positive attributes. However, many cultures around the world value unassuming behavior and silence more than talk. The Japanese do not expect their political leaders to be skillful orators (Stewart and Bennett, 1991, p. 157), and Canadian Athabaskans view quietness as evidence of knowledge and a cooperative attitude (Bowers and Flinders, 1990, p. 71). Thus, if we take silence as denoting incompetence in our students, we may be mistaken. In fact, "guarded and taciturn behaviors in the presence of teachers and/or members of the dominant culture [have] been reported of Polynesians in New Zealand, various American Indian groups . . . , Hispanics in the United States, American Blacks, and South East Asians" (Malcolm, 1989, p. 131).

In some parts of the world, students are taught to be deferential, never challenging the teacher's point of view or offering innovative ideas. For example, "Asian speech lacks individuality" (Sitaram and Cogdell, 1976, p. 119) and often conforms to tradition without trying to present something new. Furthermore, teachers may experience difficulty eliciting opinions from Korean, Japanese, Chinese, Arabic, and other students who come from school environments where rote learning is the rule. These students may even be disdainful of a professor who allows students to interrupt with questions or comments or who admits to incomplete knowledge of a subject and invites speculation from the class.

However, the opposite problem occurs in other classrooms. Mexican-American students may consider it their right to negotiate and be more autonomous in class. Some Native American (Scollon and Scollon, 1981; Philips, 1983) and Aboriginal Australian (Kearins, 1989) groups that raise their children to be independent, self-reliant, and sensitive to the differing worldviews of others will resist accepting the teacher's "correct" view without questioning. In such cultures, individuals are not only allowed but expected to interpret the meaning of events or facts for themselves.

Benefits of Small-Group Interaction

There are benefits and problems that arise when students work with their peers in small groups. Students from certain cultural backgrounds may really shine in the small-group milieu. For example, in many cultures, children do not interact directly with adults. Rather, the older children teach the younger ones. Maori students in New Zealand and students from some Native American groups in the United States may be more comfortable working with their peers with minimal direction.

In other countries where there is a hierarchical relationship between age groups (as in India among the Punjabi), it is unseemly for a younger person to disagree with or even express an opinion to an older person (Scarcella, 1990, p. 93). For students from these cultures, the critical thinking and questioning skills we hope to encourage may best be developed in small-group work, rather than in interaction with the professor, who may be seen as a respected author-ity figure who should not be questioned. Those who participate less in interac-tion with the entire class may "display great interest and competence in informal interactions with their peers" (Corson, 1992, p. 478). Malcolm notes that this pattern has been documented for students from several minority cultures, including Chicanos, Native Americans, Maori, and Aboriginal Australians.

Problems of Working Together. American students may not be able to work with one another or with international students. They may demonstrate an inability to stay on task in unsupervised groups. They may have an attitude that what they learn from each other is not of value, because they think that only the information that the teacher imparts to them and that may be found on a test is worthwhile. Hence, they may dislike working with other students in small groups.

Problems of Structure. Students who are used to rigid structure and rote learning in large classes may feel that the American classroom in general is somewhat chaotic, with too little structure. These students sometimes see only the lack of the rules they were previously expected to follow, and it may take them a while to begin to understand the subtler rules for behavior and speech that do apply.

Issues of Cooperation and Competition. Students who come from competitive societies may participate so wholeheartedly in arguing their opin-ions with the entire class that they take up too much class time. In fact, the lat-ter may see the sharing of ideas and helping one another as disruptive or as cheating (Scarcella, 1990, p. 123). In contrast, those who come from societies that value cooperation above competition may refuse to participate.

Gender Issues. Students from cultures where the sexes do not often interact, for example, the Navajo and many Muslims, may be experiencing their first coeducational schooling. These students may thus be uncomfortable working together on a project with those of the opposite sex and may work better in single-sex groups.

Student Presentations

American children are often encouraged to show off their knowledge, singing abilities, and other talents in a public display. Elsewhere in the world, children are often encouraged to be silent in the presence of adults. As a result, the lack of opportunity and cultural permission to give a formal or public presentation may later cause extreme insecurity in students when they are faced with the prospect of standing before the class and presenting their work. This anxiety is exacerbated in students who are not native speakers of Standard English because they fear that they will make grammatical errors or that their pro-nunciation will be unintelligible.

Whereas such activity may be anathema to some students, others may excel in public presentation and performance. Some African Americans, for instance, value the drama of a public narrative because of their experience with competitive and creative word-play, a style of public interaction found within certain communities. In such cases, it is also true that the dominant language may not be Standard English, so that the situation parallels that of international students, both in terms of language and culture. Such students may do well "performing" for the class if they perceive that the environment is a non-threatening one. Asian students may also have a distinctive performance style in their class presentations. "An Asian speaker makes a special effort to use lofty language . . . which is figurative and high sounding," restrained, and dignified; speeches tend to be long (Sitaram and Cogdell, 1976, p. 120). Thus, in formal situations, "Asian speech is ceremonial and highly ritualistic," and "audiences should maintain absolute silence" (p. 122).

Other cultures do not necessarily share the American style of speaking, which is problem oriented, direct, explicit, personal, and informal. The pragmatic bent toward problem solving is not shared by cultures who do not view reality as a series of obstacles to be overcome. Some Arabs, for example, see problems as "severe twists of fate that cannot be solved" (Stewart and Bennett, 1991, p. 155). Such students will not naturally adopt the basic American academic format of setting forth a problem and persuading others to concur with the proposed solution.

Americans generally expect linearity, "topic-centered presentations" (Michaels, 1981), and conciseness. The expected format for many class presentations and essays is one of getting to the point: being direct by stating the main point explicitly, followed by supporting evidence for the main idea, or the other way around. Thus, it is "*linear,* in that speakers are expected to come to the point by moving in a straight line of logical thought through the subject to an explicitly stated conclusion" (Stewart and Bennett, 1991, p. 156). One example of differing styles is that of some African Americans: the speaker talks "around" a topic rather than directly about it, and comments on ideas tangentially related to the topic (Michaels, 1981). Another style is that of the Chinese, whose presentations are more circular than linear and who write and speak discursively, coming back to the same points to show the interrelatedness of things.

The explicitness of American communication style requires clarity and specificity because ours is a "low-context culture" (Hall, 1976). Other nationalities, the Japanese, for instance, are "high-context"; that is, they rely more on the context of the situation than its content for meaning. In high-context cultures, quite a bit is left unsaid; there are many shared assumptions, and important points are likely to be made in a very subtle and indirect manner, rather than explicitly stated.

Conclusion

Only a few specific suggestions have been offered here, as it is obvious that not all techniques will work with all groups. In fact, no single strategy for classroom management can ever address the multiplicity of communication styles found among the variety of students attending American universities. Although cultural differences can interfere with classroom communication, this does not mean that we will not be able to communicate fully. Working with the kind of information presented here, knowledgeable and sympathetic professors can fully engage students in learning. Together professors and students can over-come the barriers that arise from the differing cultural norms for oral commu-nication.

References

Bowers, C. A., and Flinders, D. J. *Responsive Teaching: An Ecological Approach to Classroom Patterns of Language, Culture, and Thought.* New York: Teachers College Press, 1990. *Highly recommended for further reading.*

Corson, D. J. "Minority Cultural Values and Discourse Norms in Majority Culture Class-rooms." *Canadian Modern Language Review,* 1992, *48,* 472–496.

Hall, E. T. *Beyond Culture.* New York: Anchor Books, 1976.

Kearins, J. "They Speak English, Don't They?" In O. Garcia and R. Otheguy (eds.), *English Across Cultures, Cultures Across English.* Hawthorne, N.Y.: Mouton de Gruyter, 1989.

Malcolm, I. G. "Invisible Culture in the Classroom: Minority Pupils and the Principle of Adaptation." In O. Garcia and R. Otheguy (eds.), *English Across Cultures, Cultures Across English.* Hawthorne, N.Y.: Mouton de Gruyter, 1989.

Michaels, S. "'Sharing Time': Children's Narrative Styles and Differential Access to Literacy." *Language in Society,* 1981, *10,* 423–432.

Philips, S. U. *The Invisible Culture: Communication in Classroom and Community on the Warm Springs Indian Reservation.* White Plains, N.Y.: Longman, 1983.

Scarcella, R. *Teaching Language Minority Students in the Multicultural Classroom.* Englewood Cliffs, N.J.: Prentice Hall, 1990. *Highly recommended for further reading.*

Scollon, R., and Scollon, S. *Narrative Literacy and Face in Inter-Ethnic Communication.* Nor-wood, N.J.: Ablex, 1981.

Sitaram, K. S., and Cogdell, R. T. *Foundations of Intercultural Communication.* Columbus, Ohio: Charles E. Merrill, 1976.

Stewart, E. C., and Bennett, M. J. *American Cultural Patterns: A Cross-Cultural Perspective.* (Rev. ed.) Yarmouth, Maine: Intercultural Press, 1991.

ELLEN JOHNSON is an assistant professor in the Department of English at Western Kentucky University. She is the author of Lexical Change and Variation in the Southeastern United States, 1930–1990.

Simply assigning a paper and grading a final draft does not usually produce the kind of learning and writing that teachers desire from their students. This chapter offers strategies for working with international students throughout the writing process to produce more critical thinking and better text.

Using the "Writing Process" with Non-Native Users of English

Kimberly Koffolt, Sheryl L. Holt

Most teachers realize that a piece of writing represents only one point in a series of steps that students go through to get to a draft that is handed in to the teacher. But students, no matter what their language background, vary widely in their ability to work through the necessary steps to produce a successful paper. Fortunately, teachers do not have to resign themselves to depending solely on students' previous writing experiences. Teachers who play a more active role in guiding their students through the entire writing process of gathering ideas, organizing, drafting, and revising can help students produce writing that is thoughtful, coherent, and polished. To define "process" as applied to writing, we need to note the writing activities associated with formal writing:

- Identifying a purpose and audience for writing
- Gathering ideas
- Writing ideas down
- Clarifying and organizing those ideas
- Trying ideas out on a trial audience and receiving feedback
- Revising
- Editing and proofreading
- Sometimes starting all over as new information emerges

When working with the writing of non-native speakers, there are special considerations. It is easy to assume that weak writing by a student whose first language is not English is due to poor English skills; sometimes, however, the real problem with a poor piece of writing is not the language-related errors but the fact that the student has not met the expectations of the English-speaking academic reader in terms of audience, syntax, figures of speech, sentence

New Directions for Teaching and Learning, no. 70, Summer 1997 © Jossey-Bass Publishers

structure, and idiom. It is easier to tolerate a "foreign accent" (grammar errors) in a research paper by an international student if the paper has a clear thesis, well-developed ideas, and an effective organizational structure. Inexperienced non-native writers, however, need the opportunity to receive feedback in the preliminary stages of writing and on subsequent drafts of their papers. That feedback gives them the opportunity to correct deficiencies in content, language, and style.

By contrast, the traditional approach to giving writing assignments assumes that students come into a class already knowing effective writing strategies and that they are able to incorporate the strategies on field-specific assignments independently. But this approach makes no provisions for international students and others who have not been taught such strategies or exposed to the writing common in a particular field.

Traditional Teaching Model

The traditional approach to assigning and evaluating writing at the undergraduate level focuses on the final product, the one copy of a writing assignment that is handed in to the teacher. The instructor typically acts as both editor and judge, rarely allowing students an opportunity to rethink, rework, or expand on the paper based on feedback. The final comments and grade give international students, in particular, only a sketchy idea of what they did wrong on a particular assignment. Students who receive poor grades are unclear about how to make the writing better next time and, as a result, move on to the next writing task with little change in their understanding of what good writing entails.

Process Model

The process approach to writing, whatever the course subject matter, calls for providing an encouraging and collaborative environment within which students can work through their composing processes. The teacher's role in this approach is to help students develop useful strategies for gathering ideas on a topic, organizing ideas, drafting, revising, and editing and polishing. A crucial step in this approach is providing an opportunity for students to receive feedback on the content and organization of their papers before the final version is graded.

A teacher-guided process approach to writing assignments leads ultimately to a more satisfying educational experience for both students and teachers. Students become more successful at producing good writing, and teachers have the pleasure of noting students' progress as they read and grade better papers.

Advantages of a Process Approach for Non-Native Speakers

Although the process approach benefits all students, non-native speakers gain additional benefits. Specifically, a process approach accomplishes the following:

- *Encourages inexperienced non-native writers to begin writing early.* It usually takes non-native writers much longer than their native-speaker peers to write in English. They face two problems: (1) the pressure of a "perfect" final draft; (2) little experience with the "prewriting" and planning stages of writing. (Prewriting is the informal writing used to gather ideas before producing a final draft.) A professor can address these two problems by requiring students to produce early drafts and by giving feedback so that students can revise their work before handing in a final draft.

- *Provides feedback during the planning stage before the student invests hours on writing a long draft without a focus.* Students are very discouraged when they have spent a great deal of time writing a draft only to find out that they are not focusing the ideas adequately or are not following the expectations of the assignment. Getting feedback on a preliminary plan for a paper can head the student in the right direction on an assignment.

- *Allows non-native writers to see models of other students' writing and samples of academic writing in a particular discipline.* Despite years of English study, most international students have not been exposed to models of good academic writing in English, nor have they learned the conventions of writing in a particular field. What seems like simplistic thought may simply be "academic illiteracy."

- *Encourages feedback from peers about content, organization, and audience.* International students may sometimes bury their intelligent and unique ideas in indirect language or difficult-to-follow styles. This may occur partly due to differences among cultures in the relationship between writer and audience. Typically, an English-speaking audience admires the writer who makes the job of reading as easy as possible. In some cultures, however, the burden is more typically on the reader to ascertain the meaning behind a writer's words. International students who view the needs of their audience differently from those of a native English speaker may not want to "insult" their audience by being too explicit or direct about the points they want to make. Getting feedback from native readers helps to clarify the needs and expectations of an American audience.

- *Allows quieter international students a chance to share their ideas verbally in a small-group setting.* International students who lack confidence in their English skills or who come from cultures in which class discussion is not encouraged are often uncomfortable speaking up in a large American classroom. Unless students can meet in small groups, other classmates are deprived of the perspective these students bring to issues discussed in class and in papers.

- *Provides a much less threatening (authoritative) audience within which the student can "fail" in order to succeed in subsequent drafts.* Non-native writers are often fearful of harsh judgment from the instructor (in the form of a low grade or critical comments) and focus not so much on learning new concepts as on writing a "perfect" paper. For the international student who views the instructor as an unquestionable authority, the act of writing a paper is not necessarily an exercise in critical thinking but an act of saying what he or she thinks the teacher wants to hear.

- *Allows international students the opportunity to have someone help them with grammar editing.* Many teachers prefer that international students have a native speaker correct grammar errors before the teacher has to look at or grade an international student's paper. Although this may seem to be the primary reason for international students to share their writing with peers, it should be noted that extensive help with editing that is given too early can hinder the writing process. Once a draft is corrected, it is tempting for the non-native writer to keep the corrected version without changing the content or structure of the paper. It is also possible that international students become too dependent on native-speaker peers who cross the line of commentator to editor and writer.

Implementing the Process Approach

Teachers can encourage a process approach to writing either with in-class activities or on an individual basis. Helpful strategies for improving learning and writing using the writing process might include the following:

- Asking the student to explore the topic in advance with the instructor, the other students, or both
- Asking for a preliminary draft to be discussed with other students or the instructor
- Setting up specific grading and evaluation criteria
- Discussing sample papers in class
- Establishing documentation forms

The most useful strategies for non-native speakers seem to be encouraging prewriting, planning, peer conferencing, and multiple drafts. Although the strategies are presented here in what appears to be a logical order for a process approach, you could incorporate the strategies in any order that works for your class or for an individual student. Writing is seldom a linear activity, and it is common for writers to go back and forth among the different steps of the writing process as they complete a major writing task. You might also choose to use some of the strategies with weak writers on an individual basis and incorporate other strategies, such as conferencing and collecting multiple drafts, with the entire class.

Encourage Prewriting. One area in which you can offer guidance on the writing process is prewriting, the first stage of an assignment before students even know what they want to say. Prewriting refers to all the informal writing done on a topic to gather ideas before producing a formal draft. Encouraging students at the beginning of an assignment to use prewriting techniques such as listing and freewriting (writing ideas without worrying about organization, grammar, or development) has several benefits. For one, writing ideas informally relieves anxiety in students who put off beginning a major writing assignment for fear of not being able to write "perfectly." International students often come from educational backgrounds in which writing is used primarily for evaluation, so they think that all writing they produce must be perfect. This pressure creates a fear of writing anything until all ideas are well formed in their minds. Students who begin writing ideas down early can accomplish more when it comes time to produce a first draft than students who live with writer's block until the night before the paper is due.

Informal writing also encourages students to become not only personally invested in a topic but comfortable exploring their own ideas. This is especially valuable for international students whose native system of education may not have offered them much opportunity to express personal opinions in writing on important subjects.

You can encourage students to begin thinking and writing about an assignment with activities such as the following, which can be done outside of class:

1. Assign freewriting or journal writing shortly after giving out the assignment. Ask students to write informally on simple questions such as: "What is my topic?" "Why is this topic interesting?" "What do I already know about my topic?" "What do I think about my topic at this time?" The nonthreatening nature of these questions can yield a surprising amount of writing at an early stage. Although you are not obligated to read the responses to these questions, doing so is usually interesting and fairly easy because there is no need to worry about the form of the writing. Reading students' responses can also give you a check on how well students have understood the assignment and whether they have chosen a promising path to explore.

2. Students can be asked to list questions they need to answer in their paper or list kinds of information for which they need to search. Provide examples and encourage students to make the lists as long as they can, even if they don't end up answering all the questions.

3. Students can make up a list of all ideas and topics they think might fit in the paper. Some students will try to put these ideas in a logical order from the beginning, but more often it is best to encourage them not to develop a formal outline too soon.

4. Students can share their freewriting, journal writing, or lists with other students. Peers can respond by pointing out the most interesting ideas, asking questions, adding to the ideas, or sharing sources for more information on the topic.

Encourage Planning. Writers plan at different stages in the writing process. Some plan out the organization of ideas after they have gathered their information but before they write a draft. Others prefer to write a draft and then decide on how best to shape a revised draft. In any case, a well-written plan can be invaluable—both for student and professor—whether it is written before or after the first draft. Writing a plan with a statement of the main idea (thesis) forces students to figure out what they are trying to say in a paper; thus, reading a student's plan can be a quick way for you to check on the content and organization of a draft.

Students should be encouraged to write their plans in such a way that a reader can see a relatively complete and logical flow of ideas. At the very least, therefore, a writing plan should include a thesis statement (a one- or two-sentence summary of the main idea of the entire paper) and a logically organized list of points supporting that main idea. Writing such a plan is a difficult task for all students, but it may be even harder for international students, most of whom have never been taught how to write a formal outline. Teaching formal outlining is an option but is not absolutely necessary, because an effective plan for a paper does not have to follow the exact format of a formal outline. Furthermore, the word *plan* is not only semantically preferable to the word *outline,* especially for non-native speakers, but also functionally preferable, as it is possible to write an effective plan that does not even look like an outline.

Teaching Students How to Construct a Plan. Most students need practice constructing an effective writing plan. At the very least, they need to know what a good plan looks like. One exercise to introduce students to this skill is to take a well-written model paper and ask students to work backwards, writing the plan that might have preceded the paper. The following steps illustrate this method:

1. Hand out a sample paper (for example, a research paper, essay, or report).
2. Ask students to recreate the plan of ideas on which the paper is based. Students will need to be able to identify the main idea of the writing and the key supporting points. To encourage clarity of thought, tell students to write up the plan using complete sentences where possible.
3. Hand out your own model plan or outline of the paper after the students have completed steps 1 and 2.
4. Ask students to compare their own plan with the model.
5. Ask students to write an informal short evaluation of what they learned from the exercise. By collecting the practice plans and student evaluations a couple of times, you will have an opportunity to see the kinds of difficulties some students have reading and understanding the structure of well-written academic papers.

Using Plans Before a Draft. It is often a more effective use of time to respond to and comment on a student writer's plan of ideas than to respond to and comment on an entire draft. Students can bring an introduction plus a thesis and a plan of the paper instead of an entire draft to a peer-group conference. They could also submit these to you, perhaps on a voluntary basis, or be encouraged to bring their plans to you during your office hours.

Using Plans After a First Draft. Working with plans can be an especially efficient means of helping a weak writer after she has written a first draft. You can even avoid wading through a very weak or confusing first draft by asking a student to write down the plan of ideas that the paper contains. Often a weak draft has no underlying main point or structure. In such cases, it is more effective for the teacher and student to spend time talking through the topic. Then the students can identify and clarify the main points in an outline form rather than wasting time going through writing that has little substance or is poorly organized. When the problems of focus and organization are due to cultural differences in rhetorical style, working on a plan can help teach the student to structure the paper according to the expectations of a U.S. academic audience.

If you prefer having students work on their plans in groups, students could bring a first draft to class and be asked to "work backwards" by writing up the plan of ideas in the paper. This list of main idea (thesis) and supporting ideas can be shared with other students, who could provide feedback on the plan first and then help each other expand or improve the detail in the draft. Some teachers also ask students to read a draft of someone else's paper and try to reconstruct the plan or outline. By comparing the reader's reconstruction to the author's original plan, the author can see where he has not communicated the desired ideas clearly.

Encourage Conference Groups. One of the most useful strategies you can use to ensure better papers is to give students the opportunity to try out a draft of their ideas on a peer audience and receive feedback before revising it for a final grade. Understandably, many teachers complain that they don't have time to respond to one hundred student drafts in an effective, easy way. In fact, the burden does not have to be theirs alone. Many effective teachers have found that training students to help each other make improvements from draft to draft is time well spent. Teachers can guide students in their roles as non-judgmental critics (clarifying problems, suggesting solutions, and evaluating the results). Working in peer groups can also help students see and imitate a variety of examples without the teacher's having to produce an "ideal sample." Without the pressure of a grade, students can experiment with ideas, content, and form on first drafts, which lead, in turn, to more successful subsequent drafts. These later drafts often demonstrate that the students have learned the concepts better or show more critical thinking.

Here is a typical procedure for organizing a peer conference:

1. Students exchange copies of a first draft with two or three other conference group members.
2. At home, students comment on classmates' drafts according to specific guidelines that you have defined and presented in a handout.
3. Students meet in conference groups and discuss the strengths and weaknesses of each other's drafts. (See Nelson's chapter on problems with collaborative groups for international students.)
4. Students revise their own papers based on advice received in the conference group.

When native speakers and non-native speakers are mixed in conference groups and read each other's papers, you should help clarify the expectations for each group by discussing the awkwardness that may occur when the two groups evaluate each other's writing. You can encourage tolerance and respect by reminding native speakers that international students have worthwhile ideas and suggestions, even if they can't always communicate their thoughts perfectly in English. Remind international students that drafts by native peers may contain sophisticated grammar and vocabulary but that what might seem like perfect English does not necessarily mean the papers are well written. Non-native speakers should be encouraged to share their opinions and not be afraid to make suggestions for improving all group members' papers.

It also helps to give the groups a brief lesson on the difference between reading a paper for content and reading a paper for grammatical accuracy. Make it clear that readers should always try to read papers first for content. Readers could be told to underline language they find problematic instead of simply editing the piece. That way non-native speakers will know what to fix and will not be reluctant to revise the draft for content and organization.

Encourage Multiple Drafts. A final suggestion for encouraging a process approach in writing is to require students to hand in a folder containing not just the final draft of a writing assignment but all the prewriting, planning, and drafting that preceded the final draft. Even if you only grade the final draft, requiring students to hand in all plans and drafts encourages them to become more aware of their process and to look at plans and drafts as important. If nothing else, at least require a first draft and a revised final version.

Conclusion

Getting feedback throughout the writing process is especially helpful but often not encouraged in a college setting. Helping a student develop good writing strategies and facilitating feedback throughout the writing process will significantly improve the final product. Also, as a result of focusing on the process, students learn more content and are able to present their ideas with more evidence of critical thought. International students especially benefit from feedback on plans and drafts because they are able to try out their ideas, organizational style, and grammar on a peer audience or discuss problems with you before submitting their work for a final grade.

KIMBERLY KOFFOLT *and* SHERYL L. HOLT *teach ESL as writing instructors at the University of Minnesota in the composition program.*

Helping second-language writers develop the skill of "editing for language" is a different task from simply marking errors in a paper. This chapter focuses on strategies teachers can use to put the student writer at the center of the language editing process.

Building Editing Skills: Putting Students at the Center of the Editing Process

Robin Murie

A nineteen-year-old Vietnamese writer of English gets her term paper back from her history professor. Red circles cover the paper: verb agreement problems and missing -*ed* endings and plurals. The student glances at the markings, sighs, and stuffs the paper in her backpack. "Oh well, I guess I'm not very good at writing," she murmurs. Having arrived in the United States in junior high school, she has never really studied English formally as a language and is not familiar with much of the terminology for grammar. These language corrections are basically confusing and annoying, and they don't teach her editing skills.

A twenty-nine-year-old Chinese graduate student is struggling with a major paper for his adviser in the chemistry department. He has studied English grammar to a depth unmatched by any of his native English-speaking peers, yet his papers, too, are returned with extensive rewriting and rephrasing: prepositions, articles, odd expressions, word choice. Having lived only six months in the United States, in student housing with a group of other Chinese graduate students, he has not yet had much opportunity to build a fluent sense of idiom. He greatly fears that his major professor is dissatisfied with the English in his papers, but he hesitates to bring up the subject.

What can the professors of these two writers do to help their students become better at dealing with the language issues in their writing? What is the relationship between grammar knowledge and editing ability? How can we best help second-language writers with the inevitable language editing issues that will surface in their writing? As the title of this chapter implies, bringing

NEW DIRECTIONS FOR TEACHING AND LEARNING, no. 70, Summer 1997 © Jossey-Bass Publishers

the writer into the decision-making process is central to the strategies for building effective editing skills.

This chapter will begin with some general thoughts on language learning and the process of editing, including information from a study at the University of Minnesota looking at what students tell us about the relationship between grammar rules and editing ability. This chapter will conclude with some specific techniques that can be used to help students in our classes work with the language editing aspects of their writing.

Before proceeding any further, we need to clarify what is meant here by *editing for language. Editing* is a term often used broadly to include any kind of revising or reworking of one's writing. In this chapter, editing or *language editing* is defined narrowly to mean the kind of proofreading and reading one does for language and style issues (grammar, punctuation, word choice, typing errors). Because error is both a natural part of language learning and often a part of what marks the writing of English-as-a-second-language students, it is often of particular concern to them and their teachers.

Language Learning and the Process of Editing: Some Thoughts

The relationships among language acquisition, error correction, and grammar rules are quite complex. One's sense of language is a more powerful tool for editing than is a catalog of editing rules. The better one's "feel" for how a language sounds, the better one's ability to produce language. Therefore, what students are asked to do in our classes—read, write, discuss issues, *use* language to communicate—is absolutely appropriate. The main focus of our instruction should be on the ideas we are asking students to read and write about. In the same way, the main focus of our response to writing should be on the ideas about which students are writing. (Holt's chapter discusses the conflicts between revising for content and editing for language issues.)

Teaching grammar rules in isolation is less fruitful than discussing rules at the point at which they can be applied to an editing question. Non-native writers will gain more from information that comes in response to a specific query about a sentence in their writing than from a lecture on verb tense in a grammar class. Similarly, writers are likely to gain more from your answering their language questions than from your returning a paper to them full of unsolicited editing marks.

A sense of competence and success is important. If those "annoying circles all over the place" send a negative, shaming message to the writer, they will be counterproductive and quite possibly ignored. If the editing has been requested and is in a form that can be understood and used, it is more likely to add to the writer's sense of growth. For some writers there is a real issue of control. If the teacher moves in to point out errors, the dynamic can quickly become touchy, and the "editor" here may feel uncomfortable or choose not to look at the corrections. If the student as editor is given the pen and permission to mark areas where the English sounds questionable, while the teacher as "coach" provides information when it is requested, the editor's own ability is confirmed (because her concerns are the ones being addressed). Then a rule can be given when and where it is needed, and, most important, the writer remains at the center of the process. It does not take many repetitions of this procedure for the editor to develop a better "eye" for looking at language and editing issues.

Intuition is not enough. A non-native writer differs from a native-language writer in the range of language available from which to draw in writing. A non-native writer will not have as complete a "picture" of how the language works and is therefore likely to be more reliant on structure as a tool for language learning. (How many of us consciously learned grammar for the first time when we began studying a second language?) With native-language writers we can, to some extent, rely on time and increased fluency with written prose to solve many of the language problems that may mark novice writing, although even for native speakers there is evidence that intuition alone is not adequate. Noguchi (1991, p. 14) points out that "[t]he persistence of unconventional writing features well into the college years and even beyond suggests that editing without recognition will not work." With non-native writers, we cannot rely on this intuitive grasp of the conventions of the language to fill in the gaps.

The Relationship Between Rules and Editing Ability: Reports from an Editing Study

It is doubtful that people proofread and edit with a running catalog of explicit grammar rules in their minds. Yet when something feels odd about the "picture," having a rule to confirm the form of the verb, for example, is more useful than not having that rule. In a study (funded by the Center for the Interdisciplinary Studies of Writing at the University of Minnesota) of the editing processes of twelve Vietnamese American college freshmen in a basic writing course, there was a significant correlation between the ability to explain a given grammar rule and the ability to locate and correct grammar errors (Murie, 1995). Those who were unable to name the rules for forms of verbs were also considerably less reliable at correcting those errors in a list of sentences, both in a manipulated writing sample and in their own writing.

Teaching editing skills, however, is not the same as teaching grammar, assigning grammar workbooks, or even marking errors on papers. All of the subjects in the study had taken a grammar and writing course the previous term and had had papers marked for grammar errors by their writing instructors, but many were unable to call up a rule to help them make editing choices as they read through writing samples. The subjects were asked in a follow-up interview to talk about the relationship between learning grammar and editing well. The answers were interesting. On the one hand, they spoke of the need to know grammar, because "the ear helps, but if you don't know the rules, you don't know how to correct [the error]." On the other hand, many felt that grammar lessons without an adequate context and teacher-marked papers did not have much impact on their editing ability. As one writer in the study explained, on the chalkboard the grammar is clear, but it is another thing altogether to find the grammar error in one's own writing. Students talked about the need to apply the rules more, to connect the grammar to actual writing and editing. As one student said, "I can read grammar books, but it doesn't connect to what I'm doing when I write." Many of the students mentioned how confusing grammar rules can be. "When I learn grammar but don't work with it," a student remarked, "I forget it." In the words of another student: "If you don't practice with it, it doesn't absorb into your brain."

Having a teacher mark errors in a paper also was not useful for some of the writers in this study. One woman was particularly articulate on the subject, saying that when the teacher marks her paper, the mark is clear to the teacher, but it is not at all clear to her what the error is or what the underlying rule for that error is. This is what Hartwell (1985) referred to as COIK: an explanation that is "Clear Only If Known." The teacher knows why something is an error, but if the student does not, then a mark noting it is of little value. When a final draft is being marked, other problems also arise. As one student put it, he appreciated the feedback, but not at the point when the grade is being given: "Correct it before it is graded. I don't want the message that it's all bad." There is evidence that editing comments on final drafts are simply not well attended to. "I look for what's good," a student commented. "I ignore the other comments."

Most of the subjects in the interviews were sincerely interested in working on language issues in their writing. Several also made it clear that they considered editing to be the student's responsibility: "Don't fix the papers—make the students do the work." "Some people don't want to pay attention to their own mistakes." "It helps to have confidence in correcting your papers; students should motivate themselves more."

What the subjects in the interviews *did* want was the opportunity to work individually with a teacher or tutor. By having a "coach" who could help with editing information, and with encouragement in the process, these writers felt they could begin to make progress where textbooks, red ink, and lessons at the board had failed. Again, this points to a scenario in which the writer is at the center of the process, able to ask questions and get answers.

Knowing Who Your Students Are

Before we move to specific techniques for helping an English-as-a-second-language writer with editing issues, it is important to recognize the diversity that falls under the category of "English-as-a-second-language student." A refugee who has spent ten years in a Thai border camp and is coming to college with only four or five previous years of schooling is likely to present needs very different from those of a Chinese graduate student who has studied English intensively for fourteen years, although he has not been in a position to speak or use his English very much before now. What all English-as-a-second-language writers *will* have in common is that (1) language learning takes time; (2) language learning comes from acquiring language, not from having errors corrected; and (3) it is important to feel supported in class.

It is important to know, to the extent that you can, who your students are. How much English does this person know? How did he learn English? Was he formally taught, or did he pick it up on the playground through communication? How does he prefer to work? Some of us find grammar a fascinating subject in its own right. Others find it confusing, and they are threatened by correction from others. Does a student experience problems because

- The "picture" of English is still underdeveloped? This is someone who needs to read and communicate in English far more than she does.
- The editing knowledge is confused and incomplete? This is someone who needs to understand the verb form rules and how to locate them and check them in his writing.
- The proofreading habits are not well formed? This is someone who needs practice and confidence with the slowed-down form of reading that will catch mistakes.
- The writer has become dependent on someone else pointing out the mistakes? This is someone who needs confidence that her own voice in English communicates; perhaps this writer also needs the message that perfection is not the goal.

Given the complexity of all these variables, what can a teacher do to help an English-as-a-second-language writer build stronger editing skills and to help this writer move from being a passive recipient of our markings to a more active, more effective editor? Nelson (1991) emphasizes creating a safe place for writers to develop, a place where errors are not punished but accepted as part of the learning process; where writers are encouraged to experiment and communicate; where questions can be asked and discussed. She describes teachers who had edited to the extent that the writer's voice was silenced. In Nelson's writing center, tutors were trained to "follow the kid," to let the writers develop at their own speed. This need for "safety" points directly to the importance of placing the writer at the center of the editing process. An English-as-a-second-language writer who can be brought into the discussion at this editing stage will be in a more powerful position to effect change. Working with a writer one-on-one over time in an encouraging environment is the most effective way to provide the kinds of skills and knowledge the writer needs to become better at editing. How we do this will depend on our own circumstances: teaching load, office hours, comfort with grammar, and resources— such as writing labs—on campus.

Putting Writers at the Center of the Editing Process

The following techniques can help teachers working on language issues with English-as-a-second-language writers.

Conferencing. One of the most effective ways of putting the writer at the center of the editing process is to work alongside him in answering questions and going over a piece of writing. For those of us who have time to conference individually or in small groups with our students, this can be very effective. In its ideal form, conferencing allows the teacher to follow the writer and to note where his confusions and strengths lie. There are several advantages to this approach: it is easier to see where explanations might be useful and whether those explanations are making any sense; it builds rapport; if offered over time, it is an excellent way to help a writer develop stronger editing skills. If you alone are unable to provide this kind of work, writing centers and other places where good individualized conferencing is available can provide crucial support.

Techniques for working together orally with a student on a draft of a paper include the following:

1. *Give the student the pencil.* During a conference in which instructor and student work together to go through a piece of writing, the writer should have the pencil! On a separate piece of paper, I often keep a running list of the kinds of errors we find during the conference. This allows me to do some of the writing, without intruding on the student's paper, to illustrate a point under discussion, to list other examples of that structure, and so on. At the end of the session, we can look at this list to see what kinds of editing issues were discussed. This method allows the writer to be in control of what gets marked on the paper. It also guards against the teacher or tutor being the only active member of the conference, doing most of the writing and talking, while the writer sits quietly and nods, without necessarily understanding the gist of the correction.

2. *Ask the writer to read the draft aloud.* This can be particularly effective if the writer appears to be fairly fluent with spoken English. You can then point out when a structure is spoken correctly, even though it may not be written correctly. Note, however, that for a recent arrival to the United States with less oral proficiency, this is less likely to work effectively.

3. *Look for patterns.* As you work together on a sample of writing, pause to discuss a persistent pattern of error. Point out instances of correct usage as well. Scan the paper together for other examples of that pattern.

4. *Focus on the positive.* The focus need not always be on error. In fact, it is important to point out good uses of language—examples where a complex structure is used well, where the word choice is particularly effective, where the sentences flow smoothly. Keep in mind that error is often felt as an embarrassment. Encouragement is crucial.

Individual conferencing is the ideal but not always the most realistic alternative. There are students who would rather not discuss errors in front of their professor. We may have teaching loads that prevent us from having open office hours to the extent needed for this kind of attention. How else can we respond to editing questions in ways that the writer can learn from and feel central to the process?

Peer Editing. For professors who have their students work in small groups with drafts of papers, it is important to point out that the native English-speaking students may need some "do's and don'ts" about conferencing with English-as-a-second-language students: specifically, not to focus on language issues at the expense of the content of the paper. Peer editing can be a useful tool if it is done sensitively, with the writer in charge of the feedback. It can be intimidating if the writer is simply being corrected by another, probably monolingual student who has little awareness of what it is like to write in a second language. (See Nelson's chapter.)

Peers have some distinct advantages, however. They are not graders and thus may seem more accessible and less threatening to some writers. As native speakers of the language, they certainly have a competent "ear" for what sounds right, even if they may lack the linguistic training to offer expert language explanations. In fact, there may be times when reformulation, or rewriting a passage as a native speaker, might be more useful to demonstrate American English style than carefully crafting linguistic explanations.

Follow-Up. English-as-a-second-language writers are not likely to be able to locate all of the errors produced. The "picture" of English is simply incomplete. It will also be important for the instructor or tutor to help guide some of the editing. (See Holt's chapter for a discussion of typical grammar trouble spots and of the need to focus on a few at a time.) How one does this can vary, and here too the writers can be brought into the process. Ask the writers what they would like you to do as you read through the paper for language issues. Would they prefer to work with you in an office hour conference? Would they like you to point out one or two areas on which to work? Or to underline lightly wherever you see an error? If possible, suggest a range of options with which you are comfortable for the student to choose from.

Help the writer design effective study techniques for working on some of these language errors. Suggest that she keep a list, over time, of her more common editing issues. One error, marked once, will have less impact than notes written about a certain editing trouble spot, with examples and practice phrases to illustrate the point. Encourage language study where appropriate.

Whether you are working in a conference situation, with a paper at home, or in a situation where you are overseeing peer tutors, watch for explanations that are confusing, over-simplified, or simply not worth the work it would take to offer the rule. At times it is more appropriate to supply the correct form ("I'm not sure why it's this way, but it sounds better to me to say . . .").

Finally, and most important, do not always focus on editing. Sending the message that good writing is good communication and that the communication in a student's paper is clear can be more powerful than marking errors. Many times it is more useful to engage in discussions of content than in discussions of editing. A student jumping into research writing for the first time, for example, may be somewhat overwhelmed by the vocabulary load of the sources. This in itself can create writing with more errors. This writer may need to read more to develop more background and terminology before language editing is really appropriate. Again, let the student guide how much editing occurs. Require careful proofreading, but tolerate an "accent" in the writing.

Conclusion

When we help students edit their works, the goal is to identify trouble spots and to help the students themselves edit them. For students, knowledge of the rules of grammar and punctuation and the confidence to use them are necessary. We must also remember that students who are writing at the college level in a second or third language are language-rich, not language-deficient. In spite of their obvious errors in writing, these students are accomplished language learners, often with considerable linguistic knowledge.

References

Hartwell, P. "Grammar, Grammars, and the Teaching of Grammar." *College English,* 1985, *47,* 105–127.

Murie, R. "Insights into Editing in a Second Language: Using Verbal Report to Examine the Editing Practices of Southeast Asian Students." Unpublished study funded by the Center for Interdisciplinary Studies of Writing, University of Minnesota, 1995.

Nelson, M. W. *At the Point of Need: Teaching Basic and ESL Writers.* Portsmouth, N.H.: Boynton/Cook, 1991.

Noguchi, R. R. *Grammar and the Teaching of Writing: Limits and Possibilities.* Urbana, Ill.: National Council of Teachers of English, 1991.

ROBIN MURIE directs a one-year program for freshman non-native speakers of English at the University of Minnesota General College. She has taught ESL writing for over fifteen years, both at the University of Minnesota and the University of California at Berkeley.

Teachers often don't have the time or ability for conferencing with individual students after a draft is submitted. This chapter focuses on strategies for identifying and correcting errors in a student's draft when there is limited opportunity to meet individually with the student.

Responding to Grammar Errors

Sheryl L. Holt

One professor at my university was complaining recently about non-native writers of English. He showed me how he had gone through each of his student's papers and corrected all the grammar errors. At the end of the paper, he had written a few sentences about the arguments and overall ideas and affixed a grade. It must have taken hours to do all the corrections, but he felt that he had helped the students most by showing them their mistakes. He was certain that once they saw the corrections, they would learn from their mistakes and not make the same errors on future papers. He had approached the task of teaching writing in the same way he approached his own self-editing, based on his fairly complete knowledge of what constitutes an error and on his years of practicing the correct forms. Unfortunately, most of his students glanced over the corrections, noted the grade, and concluded that bad grammar produces a bad grade. Few, if any, went away from the paper-writing task with new strategies for writing, self-editing skills, or ideas for long-term improvement. The students had no idea whether their arguments were valid, their ideas were conveyed to the audience, or they had adequately comprehended the concepts taught in the course. They only knew that they had grammar errors on their papers and that the teacher was displeased.

What follows is meant as a guide for dealing with grammar errors in your classroom. It gives you some sense about which problems you may want to deal with and which problems are best left to trained ESL teachers. An important thing to remember is that your role as a content-area teacher is to help students become better writers in your field, whereas the task of dealing with severe grammar problems is best left to ESL writing experts.

When grading a final draft that will not be revised, the majority of the comments need to reflect content issues. It is better to pick out and comment on a few significant errors that interfere with understanding, rather than to comment on every error.

Deciding When to Focus on Grammar

Grammar errors occur in the writing of almost all non-native students. However, I am always surprised at the different tolerances that professors have for certain types of errors. What one professor thinks is serious does not seem to bother another. For instance, teachers often focus only on errors that native speakers would make—double negatives, subject-verb agreement, comma splices, run-on sentences, or spelling and punctuation errors—although these may not be the most serious problems in a paper. Before tackling the job of correction and explanation for the student, each teacher needs to decide what errors are most problematic. If the student does not have many errors that interfere with understanding, decide which problems should be worked on first and which problems can be ignored awhile. Commenting on the most seriously distracting problems first is more helpful than choosing minor, though irritating, errors.

It is also important to realize that not all students will be helped by your corrections or comments, no matter how careful you are about choosing a limited number of errors and providing adequate explanations. If grammar errors *significantly and consistently* interfere with understanding so that you cannot determine the meaning of sentences throughout the paper, then the student probably needs more help than a content professor can give. Seek options on campus such as the writing center, tutorial services, ESL classes, or peer tutoring. If possible, get advice from an ESL expert on campus so the student can be referred to appropriate resources. If nothing is available and you are willing to offer long-term help, have the student use one of the many ESL grammar and writing books and help the student work through the various exercises. (See the Reference Tools section at the end of this chapter.)

Typical English-as-a-Second-Language Errors

Sentence-level English-as-a-second-language errors are fairly consistent regardless of the language background of the student. This would seem to indicate that many errors are due to the complex structure of English rather than to the student's language-learning ability, lack of intelligence, or first-language interference. The following are the most common errors in English-as-a-second-language writing. The set of errors is not exhaustive, but it can help you isolate the various areas on which to focus your correction and explanation. With a little practice, you will be able to identify consistent areas of difficulty for students and ask them to work on a couple of areas at a time. It may be useful to mention that current computer grammar-checker programs are not very helpful for English-as-a-second-language students with these types of errors, so more of the process of identifying errors is on your shoulders.

Verbs. The verb tense system in English is complex and creates a minefield of opportunities for error. The majority of problems will probably occur with verb tenses, two-word verbs, lack of verb endings (*-ed* or *-ing*), or mixing verb forms. Students may also overuse one tense, especially the present tense or *-ing* forms. Because this is such a big area, it will not be helpful to ask the student to focus on all verb problems. It will be more helpful to look for patterns of errors. For example, many other languages do not require endings on verbs to indicate time period, but English requires considerable redundancy to do so. It is not sufficient to say, "Yesterday, I listen." We must change the verb to match the time frame. Although to native speakers it seems quite simple, to most non-native writers this is a very complex problem.

The following are some of the most common problem areas regarding verb forms:

• *Verbs following* have/has/had *require the past participle*. Examples: *they have received, he has broken, she had bought.*

• *Verbs following* have/has/had *require* to *plus a base form*. These are infinitive forms. Examples: *they have to go, she has to stop, he had to see.*

• *Verbs following* be *in the active voice*. These are in the *-ing* form. Examples: *she is going, he was singing, they will be borrowing.*

• *Verbs following* be *in the passive voice*. These are the past participles. Examples: *he was touched, they were caught, she was chosen.*

• *Past tense verbs*. These are commonly not marked or are not consistently marked. Students often use the present tense as though it were time-neutral or because it is the simplest to use ("Yesterday he go home"). Students also may not say or hear the *-ed* ending, so it is easy to forget to write it. Another problem is that *-ed* plays three different roles: past tense ("I help*ed* him"); passive voice ("The bank was robb*ed*"); and some adjectives ("The confus*ed* man changes his mind"). Students often confuse the function of these *-ed* endings.

• *Past tense choices*. We can use several forms to indicate past time (for example, *I went, I have gone, I had gone, I was going, I have been going*). Students often are confused about which of these past tenses to use in a particular context. To truly master this confusing aspect of English, students need to see a lot of examples in context and be quite advanced in their language-learning process.

• *Modal auxiliaries*. The modal (for example, *can, could, may, had better, must, will, would*) does not agree with the subject and is followed by the base form of the verb (*stand, stop, talk*), but commonly students write, "He could stopped," either trying to make the verb carry the past tense or trying to form the passive without the *be* as in "It could [be] stopped." Another possibility is that the student has forgotten or does not hear the contraction for *have* in "He could['ve] stopped."

• *Verbs followed by* -ing *or infinitive forms*. When two verbs are together, certain verbs are followed by *-ing* verbs ("I deny saying that") and others are followed by infinitive forms ("I want to go"). Others can be followed by either *-ing* or the infinitive ("He started going," "He started to go"), and some verbs change meaning depending on which form is used. An ESL grammar book or *Longman Dictionary* will list the most common verbs followed by the *-ing* or infinitive form.

• *Conditional forms.* The conditional (*would* sentences, *if* sentences, *wish* sentences) requires a fairly complex sequence of verb forms: for example, "You would have started your homework if you had been able to understand the problems." In general, conditional forms are quite difficult, and errors should be tolerated until the student has mastered easier grammatical forms. Even native speakers often make the error of saying, "If I was there" instead of "If I were there."

• *Objects.* Some verbs need an object (for example, *you, him, them*) immediately after the verb ("I tell you the truth"), whereas others do not (incorrect: "I said you"). A second-language writer may forget which verbs carry objects and which do not, so you may see "This report informs [you of] the experiment."

• *Passive voice.* Correct use of passive verb forms is a fairly sophisticated skill in English. For example, the sentence *I did the report* can be changed to a passive sentence *The report was done by me.* Students will often confuse use of the verb *be* or the *-ed* form of the verb when trying to use the passive voice, so you may see a mistake such as, "The two levels [are] equip[ed] with tables and chairs." Students may also try to use verbs such as *exist* or *happen* in the passive voice (for instance, "It can be happened.") The student should consult with an ESL expert to deal with this problem.

Other Problem Areas. The following features present their own special problems for non-native English speakers.

• *Idioms, phrases, or word choice.* Idioms such as *shoot the breeze* or *step on the gas* require students to have a fairly good ear for English, and they are often not learned in English as a Foreign Language (EFL) classrooms overseas. It is also common for international students to hear only part of an idiom or phrase or to choose the wrong word in a particular context (for example, "almost the students," instead of "almost all of the students.") Another common problem is that of having the right word but choosing the wrong form of the word (for example: *inconvenient, inconvenience; success, successful, successfully*). Simply supplying the correct word, phrase, or idiom for the student is generally an effective method; the student can thus see word choice in appropriate contexts.

• *Singular-plural agreement.* Even very advanced writers struggle with agreement problems. Many other languages do not require multiple indicators to show that something is plural. English, by contrast, does. In the following sentence, we need all of the correct plural forms for clarity: "These books are heavy." If the student says, "This book are heavy," or "These book is heavy," the reader has no priority system to determine which part of the sentence is correct. To complicate the matter, we put an *-s* on the end of verbs to indicate third person singular, but an *-s* on most nouns to indicate plural: "He works [singular] with students [plural]." Complicating the matter further is our use of collective nouns, such as in the phrase "a lot of *equipment.* Although the idea of the phrase is plural, the collective noun does not require an *-s,* and we use a singular verb ("a lot of equipment *is*"). Most international students know the rules (although they may forget which words are collective), but they need to learn to focus on agreement when editing.

• *Reduced forms.* International students who learn much of their English by ear will often have great difficulty with prepositions and other words that we "swallow" or whose sound we reduce to "a" or "uh" when we speak. ("Of" and "have" become "a" in saying "alot*a*," "should*a*," "could*a*.")

• *Prepositions.* Our use of prepositions is not consistent. We will say we are getting *on* a bus, *on* a bike, *on* a plane, *on* a train, but *in* a car. In addition, many verbs are followed by specific prepositions that follow no logic. Why do we say "he agrees *with* me" instead of "agrees *for* me"? Simply providing the correct preposition might be the most helpful if this is the area on which you want the student to focus in the paper. The student must begin a list to memorize, or establish some other systematic method for remembering the corrections. However, tolerance is probably the best strategy for prepositions until the student has more experience with English.

• *Articles.* Speakers of certain language groups such as Chinese, Korean, Japanese, and Russian often have great difficulty with articles (*the, a, an*), and it is a very difficult problem to help them overcome. Generally, it takes a trained ESL teacher to give them long-term strategies for learning. Usually, I suggest ignoring this type of error unless the student is quite proficient in English or wants to work on this area, or if it significantly interferes with understanding.

• *Sentence structure.* You may find that sentences are very short and choppy with few transitions between them, as in the following student example: "Five questionnaires were handed out. All of the questionnaires were filled out by students. The students live in my apartment. Three of them are my friends. They live in one or two bedroom apartments." Other students may have sentences that are too long and complex or are totally confusing, as in the following example: "My questionnaires were survey on eight highly regarded student consisted of four male and four female whose uses the labs quite often." Sentence structure problems make it difficult to determine the student's intended meaning and are hard to correct. If many sentence structure problems exist, writing center help or several one-on-one conferences will probably provide the only long-term solution.

Objectives for Teachers When Correcting Papers

The teacher must learn to (1) focus primarily on content; (2) isolate and explain the most significant errors first; and (3) limit the number and types of corrections per paper.

The student and professor may find several correction strategies helpful. Which approach you take may depend on the writing task, your time, or your personal preference. The strategies in this chapter focus on what you can do without the student's direct input. (For more information on teaching the student self-editing skills, with more direct, long-term student participation, see Murie's chapter on self-editing skills.)

• *Ask the students to direct the correction strategy.* Ask the students what you should focus on in the draft, or ask them to underline the words, phrases, or sentences about which they are doubtful in their own papers.

• *Read the draft two times.* On the first reading, try to understand the content and respond to the ideas with written comments. On the second reading, you can choose two or three glaring grammar areas to circle, correct, or comment on. Even very experienced ESL writing teachers often use this approach. If they begin to look at grammar too early, they soon realize that they do not know what the student is saying, and they become grammar editors too quickly. When a paper seems to have many distracting errors, make a photocopy of the draft so that you can make all grammar corrections before reading for content. This will help you focus on the content without the grammar distracting you. The student does not need to see this copy, but it helps you focus on the content alone.

• *Focus on one or two types of errors.* Focusing on one or two types of errors per paper, providing rules and focus for the student, is more useful than simply correcting or circling all errors. Many international students have a good knowledge base of English rules and parts of speech; you do not necessarily need to know all the rules, but it is important to isolate certain types of errors and provide adequate explanations and additional examples where possible. For example, if the student does not put *-ed* on adjectives in several instances, (for example, confus*ed*, interest*ed*) you could highlight all the adjectives that need to be changed. It may also be useful to point out what you are highlighting and what is missing; for example, in the margin you could write, "Many adjectives need an *-ed* ending. Look at the highlighted adjectives and see if you can correct the errors." To reinforce the pattern, find adjectives to which the student has correctly added the *-ed* ending. You do not need to highlight throughout the paper—mark maybe a paragraph or two. Making the student focus on a limited area of difficulty will help her see the repeated pattern of errors. This is not to say that the student will never make this type of error again, but it will give some focus for language learning.

• *Provide vocabulary choices and prepositions.* Admittedly, isolating a pattern of errors is not always possible or reasonable. Many language errors may not seem to have a pattern. It is difficult to isolate these areas as patterns throughout the paper. Idioms, word choice, or prepositions may simply need to be corrected for the student.

• *Highlight correct forms.* In other cases, the students have produced the correct structure in several sentences but have forgotten or ignored the correct form in other sentences. It seems that students can have difficulty focusing on the rules even though they know them. If you highlight the incorrect instances in a paragraph or two while pointing out the times when the student has produced the correct forms, she may realize that the problem is an editing issue rather than one of needing to learn a new rule.

- *Isolate one or two paragraphs.* Another strategy is to isolate a limited number of errors in a shorter section, such as a page, instead of looking at the entire piece. If one section seems to demonstrate the typical errors in the paper, it may be easier to isolate that section for comments and ignore errors in the rest of the paper. This gives you an opportunity to comment on grammar errors but does not make you focus on grammar throughout the paper. However, it is probably not helpful to correct all errors in even that shorter section. Remember that overcorrecting does not help the student focus or self-correct.
- *Distinguish between writers who have tried and those who have not.* Just as with some native-speaker writers, some non-native writers may not show any evidence of self-editing. It may seem that the student has not tried to edit or self-correct. If there is great inconsistency, ask the student to read through the draft and correct the errors he sees before you comment on the piece.
- *Tolerate some errors.* Finally, there are several types of errors that may need to be tolerated, even with advanced learners, because of the complexity of the English construction. Troublesome article and preposition errors, for example, may need to be tolerated because it takes a long time to learn how to use articles and prepositions correctly.

Grading Methods

Even if you become comfortable helping non-native writers in identifying and correcting grammar problems, grading may still be a confusing task. The question is, how can you grade the international student according to the same standards as your other students when the international student's paper still has grammar errors?

One method is to categorize what you are grading. Try using a written checklist that categorizes several areas, such as content, organization, critical thought, narrowed thesis, and grammar; put the heaviest weight of the grade on critical thought and organization. Give less weight to categories such as grammar and mechanics. In this way, if the student has very good organization and ideas, he is given credit in those categories but is graded down for grammar as only one area. This helps the student realize that the paper has several aspects that are worthwhile and that the grammar is only a (smaller) percentage of the grade. Most teachers using this method will grade down only on areas that *interfere* with understanding of thoughts. Minor problems, such as subject-verb agreement, article usage, and so on, are usually overlooked. It should be stated clearly at the outset who should help with the grammar or if you expect the student to get help at all. If outside help is seen as a form of plagiarism (another person doing work that should be done by your student), then this should be made clear.

Some instructors prefer another method. Students hand in final drafts for a grade on the due date. This draft has no penalty for grammar errors unless there is no evidence of trying to self-edit. When the paper is handed back, the student must take the paper to the writing center and correct it with the tutor.

The goal of the tutor should be to help the student find patterns of errors and give more detailed explanations, *not* to correct the draft completely. The corrected version does not change the grade but is simply an additional requirement to receive the grade. In other words, an additional corrected draft is required of the international student, but she has either not been penalized or has been penalized only slightly for grammar errors on the final draft.

Conclusion

Teaching, evaluating, and commenting on writing are more than correcting or grading poor grammar. It is much better *not* to focus on grammar until you have addressed some of the other issues—content, organization, and critical thought. Each teacher must come to some middle ground to be an effective writing and content teacher. It is not helpful to ignore or to overcorrect grammar errors. Although it may be difficult to isolate certain types of errors at first, as you become more accustomed to seeing the same types of errors over and over again in second-language writing you will become more familiar with how to identify and explain them. Ultimately, you will be able to help students learn from their errors in future drafts.

Reference Tools

The materials listed in this section are of two kinds: the first two entries are for dictionaries; the remainder are for grammar exercise books.

Advanced Learner's Dictionary of Current English. Oxford: Oxford University Press, 1974.

Longman Dictionary of American English. White Plains, N.Y.: Longman, 1983.
      Entries in these dictionaries provide information not available in other dictionaries on the grammatical requirements of different vocabulary choices. They also include simple explanations and examples of idioms along with exercises that will help with many trouble spots.

Azar, B. *Understanding and Using English Grammar.* Englewood Cliffs, N.J.: Prentice Hall, 1989.

Holschuh, L. W. *The Functions of English Grammar.* New York: St. Martin's Press, 1991.

Raimes, A. *Grammar Troublespots.* New York: St. Martin's Press, 1988.

Raimes, A. *Keys for Writers: A Brief Handbook.* Boston: Houghton Mifflin, 1996.

SHERYL L. HOLT is the composition coordinator for non-native speakers in composition courses at the University of Minnesota. She has taught ESL for twenty years.

Peer response groups contribute to students' effectiveness as writers in any field, but cultural differences in communication will affect the interactions that occur in the group.

How Cultural Differences Affect Written and Oral Communication: The Case of Peer Response Groups

Gayle L. Nelson

If students write in your classes—if they write lab reports, research papers, book reviews, book reports, summaries of articles, or any other kind of writing—consider using peer response groups. The term *peer response* refers to students' reading and responding to each other's written work to provide their peers with comments on how they can improve the draft versions of their papers. The process is similar to that of a faculty member giving a colleague a manuscript to read before submitting it for publication. The use of peer response groups is based on the premise that more emphasis needs to be placed on the process of writing and that an important component of this process is revision. In fact, there are two very practical reasons to use this method with students. One is pedagogical: peer response contributes to students becoming better writers by emphasizing the importance of revision. The other is pragmatic: peer response groups save you time, because students' papers will contain fewer errors and thus be easier to read when you receive them.

How Peer Response Groups Work

In a typical peer response group involving U.S. students, the members work in pairs or groups of three or four students who exchange course papers or assignments. The students take copies of the papers or assignments home, read them, and write comments in the margins about how the writers can improve their papers. The instructor may assign specific questions to which the readers respond, such as, "What do you think is the writer's focus?" Either during a regular class period or at a specified time and place outside of class, the students meet to discuss their reactions to each other's papers. Students then use those written and verbal comments with which they agree to rewrite their papers before turning them in to the instructor.

You may have already used this method with your U.S. students in their writing assignments. However, when we deal with English-as-a-second-language students, cultural factors may influence both the operation and the outcomes of peer response groups. If you are not aware of these factors and the cultural differences from which they arise, you may find that the groups you organize are not functioning effectively, and as a result some of the English-as-a-second-language students in your class may feel alienated and misunderstood.

Generalizations About Cultures

Because cultures differ in numerous areas, such as behaviors, communication styles, functions of language, purposes of human interaction, appropriate roles of teachers and students, and acceptable classroom behaviors, it is not surprising that misunderstandings often occur when individuals from different cultures interact. The academic field called intercultural communication investigates interactions between people from different cultures. Findings from this field provide the particular dimensions of this chapter, which were selected because they directly relate to small-group interaction and peer response groups. The dimensions are as follows:

1. Individualism and collectivism
2. Power distance
3. The concept of "face"
4. Communication style

In the final section of this chapter, I will provide possible ways to structure peer response when English-as-a-second-language students are participants.

Individualism and Collectivism. The dimension of individualism-collectivism is perhaps the best-documented dimension of variation across cultures (Hofstede, 1984; Triandis, 1988). Individualism, common in the United States, is characterized by individuals' subordinating the goals of the collective to personal goals. In individualist cultures, people are expected to take care of themselves and their immediate families and to pursue individual achievement. This focus on the individual does not imply that groups are insignificant. Members of individualist cultures frequently belong to many groups, but no specific group is responsible for one's total identity. People from individualist cultures tend to shift group membership frequently. Membership in groups depends more on personal choice, convenience, and specialization, rather than on a commitment to maintain actively the relationships that constitute the group.

In collectivism, individuals place the needs of the group above their personal needs. Unlike members of individualist cultures, collectivists belong to fewer groups, but the groups they belong to define their identity. Collectivists tend to belong to the same groups for a long period of time, if not a lifetime. Their groups provide collectivists with a sense of self-identity, with roles and norms that determine their behavior, and with a sense of purpose. A primary goal of the group is to maintain the relationships that constitute the group, to maintain cohesion and harmony among the group members. According to Hofstede (1984), collectivist countries include East Asian, Middle Eastern, and Latin and South American countries.

How do collectivism and individualism relate to peer response groups? Although collectivist cultures share the value of maintaining the relationships that constitute the group, they differ in *how* these relationships are maintained. Because I have studied students from East Asia, I will focus on them.

For students from collectivist cultures, writing groups are problematic because they often function in a way that is in opposition to the values of collectivist cultures. In most U.S. classrooms, writing groups function more often for the benefit of the individual writer than for the benefit of the group.

Using groups to focus on individual goals works with native speakers of English in U.S. educational settings because these students are accustomed to using groups to work toward individual goals. The kinds of behaviors, however, that East Asian students would normally exhibit with group members in their cultures are different from what may be expected in writing groups. For example, when interacting with members of their group, East Asians will generally work toward maintaining group harmony and mutual face-saving to maintain a state of cohesion.

Joan Carson, a colleague at Georgia State University, and I have conducted a study of three peer response groups in an ESL advanced composition class (Nelson and Carson, 1995). The purpose of the study was to provide a better understanding of how Chinese students interact with their non-Chinese peers in peer response groups. Six sessions involving three groups were videotaped. Soon after each session was recorded, an interviewer and one of the Chinese students met to view the tape and to discuss the group's interactions. Using the method of stimulated recall, the interviewer stopped the tape at regular intervals and asked the Chinese student to explain what he or she was feeling or thinking about a particular part of the interaction.

My purpose here is not to summarize the study but to point out the general patterns that emerged from the Chinese students' comments. The students reported two general areas of concern about the social dimension of the peer response group: concern for the feelings of their peers (particularly the need not to hurt or embarrass the writer) and concern for a positive group climate. One Chinese student explained why she kept her comments to herself: "I don't want to embarrass the writer or arouse an argument." The students were reluctant to criticize their peers' drafts, recognizing that making negative comments might lead to division, not cohesion, in the group. For the most part, the Chinese students were more concerned with the group's social dimensions than with providing their peers with suggestions to improve their essays. The other writers, therefore, did not have the opportunity of benefiting from the Chinese students' verbal responses to their drafts.

Power Distance. Hofstede (1984) defines power distance as a measure of interpersonal power or influence between two persons. In educational settings, power distance refers to the distance between a teacher and a student. In countries with a large power distance, teachers are treated with respect and are viewed as the holders of truth, wisdom, and knowledge. They pass this knowledge on to their students. Students perceive teachers as the ones who know, the ones from whom they will learn. They believe that the quality of their learning depends on their teachers' excellence.

According to Hofstede's research, the United States has a power distance score in the mid-to-low range. This ranking means that U.S. teachers and students are likely to treat each other as more equal than do their counterparts in countries with a larger power distance. Some countries with high power distance scores include the Philippines, Mexico, India, and Arabic-speaking countries. In a cross-cultural study comparing Egyptian and U.S. university students on items related to power distance, Egyptian students were significantly more likely than U.S. students to agree with the statement "Students expect teachers to direct their learning" (Nelson, El Bakary, and Fathi, 1996).

What does power distance have to do with peer response groups? An assumption underlying peer response groups is that students value the comments of their peers and that they believe their fellow students can help them improve their papers. If students do not value their peers' suggestions, do not consider their peers knowledgeable enough to offer useful feedback, then peer response group interaction is an empty exercise. Students from countries with a large power distance are much less likely to value their peers' views than are students from countries with a smaller power distance.

It is not uncommon for English-as-a-second-language students from countries with a large power distance to make comments such as, "I am not the teacher. I cannot say what is the right way," or "I want the teacher to tell me what to do," or "My classmates are just students like me; they don't know what is right." In one study of an ESL peer response group, all of the ESL students agreed that they did not feel competent to comment on each other's papers and that they would have liked the teacher to be part of the group (Nelson and Murphy, 1992). They wanted the teacher to tell them how to change their papers.

The Concept of "Face." The concept of "face" is often associated with the Chinese and Japanese; however, all cultures are concerned with face to varying degrees. In any social situation, those present are putting forward a particular face. The difference between the Chinese and Japanese when compared to Americans is that face has greater social significance. In China and

Japan, people are conscious of "face" most, if not all, of the time. A Chinese proverb states that "a person needs face as a tree needs bark."

In *Encountering the Chinese,* Hu and Grove (1991) set forth the basic parameters of the concept of face. Face includes each person's set of personal claims. These claims are socially and psychologically vital. One's face constitutes one's identity and generates a personal sense of integrity, dignity, and self-respect. In a social situation, all present have a stake in preserving everyone's face as well as their own. This mutual preservation of face makes it possible for social events to proceed harmoniously. Loss of face occurs when one's set of claims is called into question by another. Such a loss of face results in embarrassment for the person whose claims have been questioned and also for the person who caused another to lose face. Thus, it is a lose-lose situation: the person who caused the loss of face loses, and the person who lost face loses. The social cohesion and harmony of the social interaction is broken.

Face is also an important social construct in the Middle East. In the book *Understanding Arabs,* Nydell (1987) reports that in the Middle East, criticism can be seen as a personal insult. She advises Americans who work with Arabs to be indirect in their criticism and to include assurances of high regard for the individual. She strongly recommends that criticism not be given in front of others.

How does the concept of face relate to peer response groups? In peer response groups, students are expected to criticize the drafts of their peers' papers. This criticism can be perceived as causing the writer to lose face within the group. In the study mentioned earlier (Nelson and Carson, 1995), the Chinese students would often mention not wanting to embarrass their peers during peer response interactions. For example, one student said, "First I want to give him the encouragement; . . . I think this won't embarrass him." Another student explained that the reason she either kept her questions to herself or wrote them down was because "I don't want to embarrass the writer." And yet another said, "It's not polite to criticize." In all of these situations, the Chinese students did not want their peer to lose face in the group.

Similarly, among many Arabs, the public criticism given in peer response groups might cause the person to lose face. Nydell (1987) notes that "constructive criticism" is not translatable into Arabic and that criticism, by its very nature, is perceived as personal and destructive.

The concept of face is also related to collectivism. Both face and collectivism relate to developing and maintaining harmonious relationships in which all parties can maintain their integrity, dignity, and self-respect.

Communication Style. Communication style is an elusive notion. Loosely stated, it refers to the way we talk. Among the dimensions of communication style that have been defined and investigated, the best-documented communication style is the dimension of direct versus indirect. Americans have a more direct communication style than many other cultural groups. We value "telling it like it is," "not beating around the bush," and "getting straight to the point." We tend to be suspicious of people who do *not* say "what they're think-ing" or "what's on their minds." Chinese, Japanese, Koreans, and Egyptians, among others, have a more indirect communication style than Americans.

Like the concept of face, the direct-indirect dimension of communication style relates to individualism and collectivism. To maintain the group cohesion and harmonious interpersonal relations valued by collectivist cultures, collec-tivists use indirect means of communicating messages that may otherwise be disruptive to the group.

How does communication style relate to peer response groups? In peer response groups, differences in communication style may result in writers misunder-standing the comments of their peers and, thus, not making the changes in their drafts that are needed to improve them. For example, in peer response groups, collectivists may use indirect means to express their point of view. Instead of saying, "I think you need to omit this example because it doesn't relate to your main idea," a student from a collectivist culture may say, "Why did you include this example?" To this question, the writer may simply explain why that example was used. The results of research with Chinese students (Nelson and Carson, 1995) suggest that Chinese students are not likely to fol-low up on such a response to a question, thus leaving it to the writer to decide if the question meant anything more than appeared on the surface.

Recommendations

In this chapter, I have noted four dimensions of intercultural communication that affect peer response in group interactions. Considering these intercultural issues, what are some effective ways to use peer response in classes that include English-as-a-second-language students?

One way is to ask students to work in pairs instead of small groups. The interactions between individuals in pairs are not as complex as the interactions in groups, and an English-as-a-second-language student is less likely to lose face if only one other student is present. An example of how to implement peer response using pairs is given here.

1. Explain the purpose of peer response: for students to read and respond to each other's writing so that students can see their writing through the eyes of the readers and can use the readers' comments to revise their drafts.
2. Ask students to bring in extra copies of their papers and give them to their partners.
3. Ask students to read and respond in writing to their classmates' papers by a specified time.
4. Ask students to meet with their partners—either in or outside of class—to discuss each other's papers and elaborate on their written comments.
5. Explain that when students finish discussing the papers, they should return them to the writers with written comments.

6. Ask writers to listen to and consider their partners' suggestions but to remember that they are the writers and they make the final decisions about how to write their papers.

A second way is to group speakers of the same language and cultural background together, as they will better understand the nuances and subtleties of each other's messages. Whether you use pairs or groups, you can use the procedure just described. With groups, however, students will need to bring in multiple copies of their papers.

It is also possible to use peer response groups that include both U.S. native speakers of English and English-as-a-second-language students, particularly if you provide additional training in peer response procedures and interactions. Inform your U.S. native speakers of English about cultural differences in group interaction patterns, group functions, communication styles, and the concept of face. (Some students may even want to read this chapter.) By being informed of cultural differences in communication, they may be better able to interpret the feedback they receive from the English-as-a-second-language students and also better able to provide those students with effective feedback.

Before concluding, I must point out the importance of training all students in appropriate peer response behavior. One set of guidelines explaining how students are expected to interact with each other before and during peer response is provided here. These guidelines are a modified version of those used in the composition program at the University of Minnesota.

The student who is *reading* a peer's paper is expected to do the following:

1. First read the paper for content and meaning.
2. Reread the paper and write down reactions, comments, and suggestions for improvement.
3. Talk to the writer about reactions to and suggestions for his or her paper.
4. Do not disagree with another reader's comments.
5. Be prepared. Fellow students depend on each other's contributions.

Writers often have specific questions or concerns about their papers. If so, they can begin their dialogues with the readers by writing questions on their papers. For example, a student may write, "I'm not sure I like my conclusion. Do you have any ideas about how I can improve it?"

During the interactions between writers and readers, the *writer* needs to do the following:

1. Be attentive and listen carefully to the readers' comments.
2. Do not argue with or reject the readers' comments.
3. Do not justify the decisions he or she made as a writer.
4. Remember that comments made by readers are suggestions and that it is up to the writer to decide which suggestions to use and which ones not to use.

Conclusion

Peer response may not be an appropriate technique for all writing situations. For example, a faculty member in social work informed me that in her class, students write on the same topic. She was concerned that if students read each other's papers, they might take someone else's ideas and put them in their own papers.

For many writing situations, however, peer response is an effective technique that benefits students and instructors. It is useful in classes consisting of native speakers of English and in classes consisting of both native speakers of English and English-as-a-second-language students. If your class includes English-as-a-second-language students, the interactions that occur in peer response groups will be influenced by the students' cultures. Thus, students need some training in intercultural communication. By addressing the cultural issues head-on and informing your students about cultural differences in communication, you can improve peer response interaction and also contribute to your students' understanding of other cultures.

References

Hofstede, G. *Culture's Consequences: International Differences in Work-Related Values.* Thousand Oaks, Calif.: Sage, 1984.

Hu, W., and Grove, C. *Encountering the Chinese: A Guide for Americans.* Yarmouth, Maine: Intercultural Press, 1991.

Nelson, G. L., and Carson, J. G. "Social Dimensions of Second Language Writing Instruction: Peer Response Groups as Cultural Context." In D. Rubin (ed.), *Composing Social Identity in Written Language.* Hillsdale, N.J.: Erlbaum, 1995.

Nelson, G. L., El Bakary, W., and Fathi, M. "A Cross-Cultural Study of Egyptian and U.S. Education Based on Hofstede's Four-Dimensional Model of Cultural Differences." *International Education,* 1996, *26* (1), 56–76.

Nelson, G. L., and Murphy, J. "An L2 Writing Group: Task and Social Dimensions." *Journal of Second Language Writing,* 1992, *1,* (3), 171–193.

Nydell, M. K. *Understanding Arabs: A Guide for Westerners.* Yarmouth, Maine: Intercultural Press, 1987.

Triandis, H. C. "Collectivism vs. Individualism: A Reconceptualization of a Basic Concept in Cross-Cultural Social Psychology." In G. K. Verma and C. Bagley (eds.), *Personality, Cognition, and Values: Cross-Cultural Perspectives on Childhood and Adolescence.* London: Macmillan, 1988.

GAYLE L. NELSON is an associate professor of applied linguistics and ESL at Georgia State University in Atlanta. She received her Ph.D. in intercultural communication from the University of Minnesota.

After discussing why and how to involve non-native speakers in
classroom talk, this chapter cautions against pressuring Asian
immigrant students to adopt American speech habits that may
threaten their Asian-language identities.

Please Speak Up:
Asian Immigrant Students in
American College Classrooms

Barbara D. Hodne

During the years I taught college-level English as a Second Language (ESL), I often tried to visualize my students in the math, sociology, or economics classes they took as they completed our courses. When I asked a Vietnamese student whether she was meeting native speakers in her math class and what it was like studying with them, she said, "I haven't met anyone. No one talks. Before class, the Americans all sit and read *The Daily,* and then we listen to the lecture." At home, I asked my son whether he had met Asian students in his calculus class. He said, "No, they sit together and talk in their own languages." In this scenario, ESL students and their native-speaking classmates move through their freshman and sophomore years on parallel tracks, not engaging each other in either social or academic discourse. We as instructors have the power to change those dynamics by providing—during or outside of class—non-threatening, task-oriented openings for one-to-one contact with faculty, teaching assistants, and classmates. But as we do so, we must also be aware that adopting American language habits may cause Asian immigrant students real anxiety about losing or giving up their Asian language habits. Fluency in social interaction can threaten the identities our students developed in their home countries.

Conversation Is an Academic Skill

On the surface, the social distance between immigrant students and their native-speaking classmates seems benign, but it has its dark side. A 1990 report commissioned by the California State University (CSU) system found that of all the minority groups represented in the CSU system, Asian Pacific Americans have been the least satisfied; for them, the stress of adjusting to a rigorous academic load is compounded not only by language difficulties but also by cultural differences, value conflicts, and both subtle and overt racism (Asian Pacific American Education Advisory Committee, 1990, p. 12). These stresses are, of course, interrelated: any curriculum, rigorous or otherwise, is more challenging in a second language; language learning is inhibited by culture shock; cultural adjustment is thwarted in hostile environments, and so on. The challenges are not specific to California classrooms, as is clear from interviews with Massachusetts ESL students who characterized American college classrooms as places "that silenced them, that made them feel fearful and inadequate, that limited possibilities for engagement, involvement, inclusion" (Zamel, 1995, p. 512). Easing the way for oral communication may be an important first step in integrating Asian immigrant students on our campuses.

But comfortable integration is not the only or even the most important consideration. Immigrant students must speak English fluently because advancing in higher education may depend on verbal ability; one former student of mine whose 4.0 grade point average qualified her for early admission to the University of Minnesota's School of Dentistry was asked to wait a year and improve her speaking skills before doing clinical work. Similar situations occur for job seekers who have impressive grades on their transcripts, and degrees in hand. While trying to make a good impression they may be seen as less qualified or less intelligent if their English is flawed. Clearly, there are very real barriers for those lacking oral communication skills.

Debra Lee's chapter shows how teachers can make their oral communication more understandable to English-as-a-second-language students. However, ensuring that students understand *us* is only half of the work. We must create an environment in which students can successfully make themselves understood. English-as-a-second-language students express hopes that they will find patient, tolerant, and encouraging teachers who pay attention to them and work toward communication (Zamel, 1995, p. 511). Significantly, teachers who fail to provide this encouragement may be seen as prejudiced against immigrants. When asked whether their public school teachers treated them unfairly because of language or nationality, more than one-third of California immigrant students interviewed said yes and explained by saying that their teachers avoided students because of language difficulties (Olsen, 1988, p. 65). Non-native speakers may have great difficulty making the first move, though; they risk confusion and embarrassment if teachers misunderstand them, and it is even worse when their classmates misperceive, ignore, or ridicule them.

Provide Opportunities for Talk

In the last twenty years, the understanding that language develops globally, that students benefit most from classes that draw on all four language skills (reading, writing, listening, and speaking), has led teachers at all levels to integrate multiple language modes in their curriculum (Rigg and Allen, 1989, p. xi). Now, workshops on writing across the curriculum coach us on how to exploit the kind of thinking students do when they grapple with ideas on paper; we coach from the sidelines while students lead discussions in which *they* clarify or synthesize course material; business courses require students to write in groups, their final papers reflecting collaborative reading, discussion, and writing. Innovative teaching techniques increasingly guide students to develop broader academic-language skills through practice and experimentation with listening, speaking, reading, and writing in the academic style. Classroom talk is an important vehicle for rehearsing that style.

Initiate Informal Conversations. Even if your curriculum commits you to a lecture format, it is worth remembering that informal, one-on-one contact with faculty outside of class may be the single most important factor in retaining Asian and Pacific American students in college (Asian Pacific American Education Advisory Committee, 1990, p. 15). Provide nonthreatening reasons for students to see you during office hours (for example, to pick up a supplemental handout), or perhaps enter from the back of the auditorium and stop to talk to individual students for a moment; whatever your approach, find ways to invite informal contact. Such encounters are less risky for you and your students than the usual question-and-answer period in lecture classes. This way, you can get used to non-native speakers' accents in private conversation and avoid the publicly embarrassing misunderstandings that students dread so much. You also will be better prepared to paraphrase a non-native speaker's contribution to discussion, thus mediating for classmates who may not yet understand the student's accent. Assigning group projects and encouraging study groups are other ways to encourage meaningful contact with you, your teaching assistants, and other students outside of class.

Involve More Students in Class Discussion. Quiet students—whether native or non-native speakers—may be more willing to speak up if you minimize their risks. One technique is to begin the discussion with open-ended questions such as, "What do you remember most from the reading?" Give students a few minutes to write in response to a question before class discussion begins. Ask them to compare their responses in pairs or small groups and report to the class. Encourage them to refer to their written responses during the discussion (Davis, 1993, pp. 78–79). A variation on this is to hand out discussion questions on cards, allow pairs of students time to prepare answers, and then work those questions into the discussion. These techniques assure students that they will not be caught unprepared. And if you allow students the right to decline an invitation to speak (and coach them to say, "I'll pass this time" or "I'm not prepared to speak right now"), you have an even better chance of achieving the nonthreatening atmosphere most conducive to whole-class discussion (Scarcella, 1990, p. 95).

Structure Small-Group Communication. Ideally, informal exchanges among students in small groups offer great opportunities for non-native speakers to join classroom talk; in practice, though, these are often times when English-as-a-second-language students feel most vulnerable and misunderstood. One Vietnamese student felt that American students misinterpret non-native speakers' quietness; she wrote that when Asian immigrant students "do not understand nor have enough English to express their ideas, . . . instead of answering questions, they smile. Being afraid of wasting the time of group they do not dare to ask for explanation. . . . Day to day, the quietness of immigrant students became familiar and common. Gradually the stereotype that they are 'lazy, impolite, uncooperative, and unfriendly' is formed."

A similar communication breakdown between native and non-native speakers was captured on film for a cross-cultural sensitivity program. In the course of a conversation, an American student asks one question after another, and a Vietnamese student responds with one brief answer after another. Each expresses frustration afterward, the American because the Vietnamese showed little interest in the conversation, and the Vietnamese because the American "kept firing questions at her without giving her time to respond" (cited in Scarcella, 1990, p. 103). Based on their differing expectations about how quickly the conversation ought to proceed, each perceived the other's behavior as uncooperative.

To prevent communication breakdowns like these, coach students on how communication styles can be misinterpreted and give them strategies for cooperation and turn-taking (Scarcella, 1990, p. 105). When students move to small groups, let them know you expect the more vocal students to hold back a bit and the more reticent students to contribute. You might ask them to begin by telling other group members whether they tend to be a talker or a listener. Some teachers ask students to use a checklist to record the number of contributions each member makes; others ask groups to designate a leader (to keep the group on task), a diplomat (to help mediate disputes), and a recorder (to take notes). Although these roles are defined, they also allow for individual styles.

Understand the Tensions in Changing One's Speech Style

Once you establish your classroom as a nonthreatening environment, another and deeper layer of tension remains: a student's mastering academic discourse means changing the style and content of her speech, which may in turn result in her being accepted by the new group but alienated from the old one (Bizzell, 1986; Dews and Law, 1995). Working-class and ethnic minority students who have "made it" often look back and remember feeling that their Black English, rural accents, or working-class speech styles marked them as outsiders in college, and that once they had acquired the vocabulary and pronunciation favored at college, membership in their home communities was threatened. We sometimes forget that non-native speakers acquiring English face equal or greater threats to their linguistic identities.

As we encourage our Asian immigrant students to "speak up" in class, we must also be aware of the strain that acquiring competency in spoken English may exert on their native-language values and behaviors. Guides to cross-cultural communication often use lighthearted anecdotes to explain differences in gestures and body language; travel guides remind us that the circle Americans form with the thumb and forefinger to gesture "perfect" or "exactly" is an obscene gesture for South Americans. In a more serious vein, educational researchers warn that patterns for eye contact differ across cultures and that in most American Indian societies listeners signal their attention by averting their eyes, a pattern often misunderstood by non-Indian teachers. Many of these researchers seem to assume that once we are conscious of the differences, we simply need to be careful and we will avoid misunderstandings. It is less common to hear people describe their uncomfortable, step-by-step experiments in acquiring a new speech style and body language.

In one training seminar I attended, my colleagues and I watched a videotape in which a seminar member conferred with a Vietnamese student about a paper she had written. He loudly dominated the conversation and finally provoked the student to defend her paper. Afterward, he acknowledged that his approach was aggressive, but said that at least he had gotten her to speak up for herself. In another meeting, a teacher who had included "participation in class discussions" in her grading scheme was asked whether this might disadvantage shy or quiet students or perhaps the non-native speakers in the class. She replied, "They need to learn to speak up. They won't learn if they don't get involved." In this view, quiet students lack self-confidence; they have a character defect that requires correction.

When colleagues express this idea, I tell the story of a Cambodian man who sat in my office and tearfully told me about a telephone conversation of a few days before. He had answered the phone (speaking in Cambodian), but heard only silence on the other end before the caller hung up. A moment later, the phone rang again, and when he answered, his friend asked (in Cambodian), "Leong, is that you? You sound different." On one level, this is a success story. At the beginning of the term, Leong had found it very difficult to add his voice to class discussion—we could not hear him. Now, to my American ear, he was simply speaking more audibly. But in his view, this story showed much more profound changes: in "speaking up" as his teachers encouraged him to do, he felt that he was losing the gentle, soft-spoken voice Cambodian people cultivate and value.

Writing about Asian students in American colleges, some of my students supplemented their research with anecdotes from personal experience, particularly anecdotes about their speech class and the problems it presented for a classmate recently arrived from Vietnam. One paper discussed the flustered moment when the student slipped into Vietnamese; another analyzed his feelings as he tried to join class discussions. Yet another reported that Thanh was receiving low grades because he couldn't meet the teacher's criteria for an effective speech; that is, he was not using eye contact and gestures to engage the audience and emphasize important points. The moral of the story, as drawn by Thanh's classmate, was that "if a student keeps tight to their culture and can not adapt to new culture, that student hardly does well in college." In their debates about the relative justice or injustice of these grading criteria, what was at issue was a non-native speaker's willingness or ability to adopt a new persona to fit the new language. For Thanh and Leong, fluency in social interaction with Americans came at the cost of anxiety about losing native-language norms.

Speaking up in class need not mean a radical shift in persona. With more explicit negotiation of cultural differences, Thanh might have learned to make his own speech style work in the American context by using handouts or other visuals to reduce the need for eye contact. Similarly, even when "class participation" is included in a teacher's grading criteria, a student like Leong could meet the requirement by working in a small group or in pairs, where his quiet voice might even be appreciated.

Allow for Multiple Worldviews

American academic culture directly challenges the social ethics that many Asian immigrant students bring to their American classrooms. We measure maturity and intelligence by the extent to which students are willing to weigh alternatives and ally themselves with one stand or another only after careful deliberation (Bizzell, 1986, p. 299). Using this interpretive framework, we may see Asian students' respect for community, tradition, and authority as naive and unsophisticated. The result is that Asian immigrants feel, as many working-class and ethnic-minority students do, that "they are being asked to abandon their less prestigious, less socially powerful world views in favor of the academic" (Bizzell, 1986, p. 299). Ironically, we also benefit from Asian students' altruism and appreciate the deference with which they approach us, often interpreting it as deep respect because conventional wisdom has it that Southeast Asians revere teachers. But Asian immigrant students I have known rigorously evaluated their teachers' dedication. Their critiques of American educators challenge us to build a more unified ethic and earn their deeper respect.

In her chapter, Gayle Nelson warns that students from collectivist cultures bring very different assumptions and practices to what we call collaborative learning; they may surprise or even disconcert us by accepting responsibility for the success or failure of members of their group. I was appalled the first time I saw a student set aside two weeks of research and start over with a new paper topic so she could help a young man who was two weeks behind and struggling to catch up. I had advocated collaboration since the first week of class but was perplexed by her decision—did she not realize that she herself would now fall behind in her work? She explained how important it is for older, more successful students to help those who are younger and less successful.

A few years ago, I sat with a student and suggested revisions for a paper in which he had written, "Teachers are unselfish people who give their whole lives to their students. Money means nothing to them, they only think of the good of the students." Believing that this simple, formulaic statement reflected superficial rather than critical thinking, I suggested he consider the topic more deeply; he might read about teacher burnout, complaints about workload, resentment about salary freezes, and the tensions between faculty and administration. From the horrified look on his face and the stories he told about his teachers in Vietnam, I realized that this man was not a superficial thinker; rather, critical thinking about teacher-student relations may yield a different result in Vietnam than it does in the United States.

A Linguistic Middle Way

When immigrant families in the United States encourage their children to learn English, the parents often shift away from actively teaching or maintaining the language of their home country; the two languages "appear to be competing for limited linguistic space, so that the primary outcome is displacement" (Hakuta, 1986, p. 167). Classrooms have usually been the place where children of immigrants shift their allegiances to American culture and American English. Some observers see this shift as successful integration into American society; for them, it shows the American melting pot at work. Others point to the psychological stresses that children experience when their home languages are not valued or developed at school; they argue for bilingual education programs that promote acculturation but do not suppress languages other than English. Such discussions inevitably focus on children; presumably, college-level English-as-a-second-language students are seen as secure in their cultural and linguistic identities.

As the anecdotes in this chapter show, however, Asian immigrant students in U.S. colleges feel a similar linguistic alienation, with pressure to give up the language habits of their home countries in favor of the body language, speech style, and intellectual stance of American academia.

In helping students become secure in the culture and language of the academy, we can provide nonthreatening opportunities for informal conversations and whole-class discussions. Such opportunities can encourage international students to recognize that they do not need to abandon their native languages to become successful students.

References

Asian Pacific American Education Advisory Committee. *Enriching California's Future: Asian Pacific Americans in the CSU*. Office of the Chancellor, California State University, Long Beach, Calif., Nov. 1990. (ED 348 914)

Bizzell, P. "What Happens When Basic Writers Come to College?" *College Composition and Communication,* 1986, 37 (3), 294–301.

Davis, B. G. *Tools for Teaching.* San Francisco: Jossey-Bass, 1993.

Dews, C. L., and Law, C. (eds.). *This Fine Place So Far from Home.* Philadelphia: Temple University Press, 1995.

Hakuta, K. *Mirror of Language: The Debate on Bilingualism.* New York: Basic Books, 1986.

Olsen, L. *Crossing the Schoolhouse Border: Immigrant Students and the California Public Schools.* San Francisco: California Tomorrow, 1988.

Rigg, P., and Allen, V. G. *When They Don't All Speak English: Integrating the ESL Student into the Regular Classroom.* Urbana, Ill.: National Council of Teachers of English, 1989.

Scarcella, R. *Teaching Language Minority Students in the Multicultural Classroom.* Englewood Cliffs, N.J.: Prentice Hall, 1990.

Zamel, V. "Strangers in Academia: The Experiences of Faculty and ESL Students Across the Curriculum." *College Composition and Communication,* 1995, *46* (4), 506–521.

BARBARA D. HODNE is assistant professor of English at Sonoma State University. She taught college-level ESL writing from 1987 to 1995 at the University of Minnesota in a program that primarily served Southeast Asian immigrants and refugees.

International students identified problems in the classroom that hindered their learning. These included listening difficulties, lack of understanding of differences in cultural backgrounds, poor oral communication skills, insufficient vocabulary, and poor writing skills. The students suggest ways professors can help them overcome these problems.

What Teachers Can Do to Relieve Problems Identified by International Students

Debra S. Lee

International students face many challenges when they arrive in the United States. Not the least of these is how to become fully functioning participants in a classroom at an American academic institution. You can enhance international students' ability to participate fully in the classroom by following some of the suggestions offered by the international students themselves. Following their suggestions does not mean requiring less of them than you do of American students. However, you can ease their transition to an alien academic system by recognizing the problems they have in your classroom.

This chapter is devoted to problems the students have identified and to their proposed solutions. Before we begin, however, we must identify the students.

International students: Who are they? Do all of them speak English as their second, third, or fourth language? Although as a group international students can include native English speakers—Canadians, for example—these students do not have as many problems in the classroom as do international students whose native language is not English. This chapter addresses the language problems of this latter group of international students or of those whose variations of English differ considerably from the American norm (see the chapters by Stalker and Johnson on the varieties of native English).

As part of a group project in a language skills class, international graduate students from various disciplines were asked to identify the top five problems they experienced in the classroom and to provide solutions for them. The students participating in the project were first- and second-semester graduate students, so the issues they identified are weighted for areas of concern to relative newcomers. The international students in the project accepted primary responsibility for solving communication problems. They recognized the need to adjust to the American-type classroom, which includes, among other things, more interaction between professors and students, smaller classes, a more explicit writing style, idiomatic language in spoken and written English, and a less formal classroom structure. According to the students, however, professors can help alleviate some of the problems. The issues identified by the students include the following:

- Listening ability
- Differences in cultural background
- Oral communication skills
- Vocabulary
- Writing

Listening Ability

For first- and even second-semester international students, the inability to understand the professor and fellow classmates can be debilitating. (Students who have been in the United States longer than two semesters report a lessening of this problem.) Two of the primary causes of listening problems are (1) that students often learn British English from teachers who are non-native speakers, so that their prior experience with spoken English is not with American English; and (2) native English speakers' use of idiomatic language (*a ballpark figure,* for example; see Maylath's chapter) and reduced forms (*gonna* for *going to, wanna* for *want to*; see Holt's chapter).

So how can you help students with their listening difficulties? International students have offered the following suggestions:

1. *Professors should speak slowly and clearly.* By reducing the speed of your speaking even a little, you are giving the students a chance to absorb what you say. American students, as well as international students, can benefit from a slower rate of speed—it is easier to take notes and follow the discussion or lecture. You do not have to cut your rate of speech in half; simply become aware of the speed and slow down as much as possible.

2. *Repeat key terms and write them on the board.* Adapt ESL techniques for use in your classes. Boardwork and repetition are essential in ESL classrooms and can be used to aid any student. Repeating key terms, writing terms on the board, or preparing a handout helps students (both international and American) follow the lecture. Some professors have a section of the blackboard set aside for key terms and daily plans that they complete prior to class. This gives students a baseline to follow if they lose the thread of the discussion.

3. *Write homework assignments on the board or use a handout.* When students have trouble following the lecture, they may not understand oral assignments, due dates, or changes to assignments. International students are

extremely concerned about the possibility of missing assignments and losing credit—not because they could not do the work or simply did not do it—but because they did not know that it was due.

Remember that asking if everyone understands the assignment or knows when it is due may not be enough. International students may be too embarrassed to speak up or may not even understand that you are discussing an assignment. When I first began teaching ESL, I made an oral change to a due date and did not follow through by writing the change on the board. When I asked if everyone understood, no one said a word. However, a Chinese student, who had only been in the country four days, did not understand and later was extremely embarrassed when he did not have the assignment prepared when due. As I knew that oral amendments could create problems for international students, his embarrassment was my fault.

4. *Provide copies of notes or make clear which sections of the book are being covered each day (or both).* If possible, offer to provide copies of notes for students to review at home or point out areas of the text (or additional texts) for students to study. Often students (not just international students) who do not understand the lecture go home and try to learn class discussion material by reviewing the textbook.

International students are often shocked to discover that professors do not begin at chapter one and continue through the book and that they use outside material for classroom discussions. The tendency of American professors to modify textbooks and use outside sources to develop a unique class design creates obstacles for students who have listening difficulties. Access to notes or a list of helpful outside sources helps the students keep up with the class.

5. *Recommend that international students listen to news programs on television or the radio.* Most students are aware of the need to listen to television and radio. What they often do, however, is use the closed-caption viewing subtext on the television in the mistaken belief that this helps listening comprehension. With closed captions, students are practicing reading skills, not listening skills.

Listening to the radio, such as the local National Public Radio (NPR) station, is more helpful for improving listening skills. If the students tape the program they are listening to, they can repeat the tape until they are certain that they understand the material. Five-minute news summaries on NPR are an excellent way to begin listening practice.

Cultural Background Differences

International students consider cultural background differences a major hindrance in the classroom, particularly when professors use "Americentric" examples to explain concepts. Students who are unfamiliar with the examples may not understand the concept and so have additional information to decipher.

Often American students from other parts of the country have similar problems if regional examples are being used. These American students, however, are more likely to ask questions than international students, who think that everyone else in the class understands the example and that it is simply their language skill that is causing the problem. International students have recommended the following courses of action to help them.

1. *Provide background information.* Take a few minutes to provide brief background information about companies, locations, or ideas. For example, an international business student from Taiwan described being asked to do a project comparing marketing styles of Kroger and Piggly Wiggly. He had no idea that the two stores were local supermarket chains. Therefore, before he could begin the project, he had to do library research to determine what types of stores these were. Did they manufacture steel or pharmaceuticals, or were they department stores?

Remember that what is everyday and commonplace to you may be an alien company, concept, or location to international or American students in your classroom. What if you were asked to compare the companies Wei-Chuan and Wei-Wong in Taiwan? You might be able to guess that the two companies were competing chains from the word "Wei," but what is their product? Most of you would have no basis for a guess and would start at "ground zero," far behind the Taiwanese students who already know that Wei-Chuan and Wei-Wong are competing supermarket chains in Taiwan.

2. *Recommend magazines or books for library research.* The students will conduct library research for culturally specific assignments. Help them by recommending specific books or articles. Remember that all the "catching up" your international students are doing is in addition to other classwork, and a brief explanation of Americentric concepts can be tremendously helpful.

3. *Recognize that students are probably suffering from culture shock.* No matter how much international students want to study in the United States, they certainly suffer culture shock on arrival, and it may last anywhere from the first few months up to two years or more of their stay in the country.

One form of culture shock is a feeling of discomfort in the classroom. A Thai student reported that he was extremely uncomfortable in graduate business classes because the students called the professors by their first names. In his culture this is a sign of disrespect; teachers in Thailand are respected authority figures and are always addressed with an honorific title, such as "Teacher." This same student also expressed shock at the students' questioning of professors, which is considered impolite in Thailand.

How can you tell if a student is in culture shock or distress if she comes to your office? In general terms, if the student has been in the United States only one or two semesters and comes to your office, you can assume that she is in distress. How can you help this student? The international students themselves suggested the first method, and three additional suggestions have been added that might prove useful.

• *Spend time with the students.* Many international students come to your office only if totally confused, because they are uncertain of the welcome they will receive and because questioning a professor can be an implied insult of the professor's ability to explain the material. To help alleviate this confusion, spend a little extra time with the student. Take ten to fifteen minutes to explain an assignment and ask the student to come back if he has more questions. If you don't have time when the student comes by, make an appointment for a later date.

A perception on the part of the student that you are unwilling to help causes you to lose a participant in your classroom. For example, a Taiwanese student sought help from a professor during his first semester on campus only to be told that he needed to attend the intensive English institute to improve his English skills. The student, who was having trouble understanding the professor, needed a little more of the professor's time, not a semester in the English institute. The student took a risk by going to see the professor and gained nothing but a loss of self-respect, so he never went to see the professor again; the professor lost valuable insights from a Taiwanese perspective for a management seminar.

• *Make clear what constitutes good writing in your class.* Different cultures have different notions of what is good writing. What appears to be an incomplete, vague paper to you as an American may be a brilliant paper in China, Japan, or Germany.

• *Recognize that international students may ascribe a different connotation to a word than the one you intend.* In one instance, Egyptian students misunderstood the importance of higher scores on an English proficiency exam because the instructor told them that the exam was like a puzzle or a game. To an Egyptian, a game is something unimportant; to the instructor it meant that the exam scores could be improved with test-taking strategies and by being calm on exam day.

• *Have the student explain the assignment in her own words either orally or in writing.* To see if the student understands an assignment, have the student explain what you have said in her own words. Does it appear that the student gives the same importance to various aspects of the lecture or assignment that you do? Although it may seem like you are being asked to spend too much time with international students, consider the benefits and insights they can bring to your classroom, such as a global perspective, cross-cultural training, and new ways of thinking about a problem. However, you can take advantage of the knowledge brought to the classroom by your international students only if they are fully functioning members of the class.

Oral Communication Skills

International students view their oral communication skills as a serious impediment to full class participation. Embarrassment and imported cultural norms operate together to keep international students from asking questions or participating in class discussions. Students reported that lack of confidence in their oral skills (based on lack of peer understanding) keeps them from speaking up in class. This is a particularly serious handicap in seminar classes in which class participation is often part of the grade. Student suggestions for assistance are as follows:

1. *Provide review questions.* Students requested sample review questions so they could try to anticipate the direction the class would go and prepare responses in advance. This is one of the least practical of the suggestions because it is often difficult to predict the direction a classroom discussion will take, and prepared responses may be inappropriate.

2. *Provide an atmosphere conducive to questions.* What can you do if you don't understand the international students' questions? Even if you encourage questions in class, how can the international students participate when the other students do not understand what they say? You can provide an atmosphere conducive to questions from international students by following some of their suggestions.

• *Listen carefully and make an educated guess.* International students are easier to understand the more often you listen to them. Additionally, you often understand more than you think you do. For example, when watching a videotape of an international student, professors frequently say that they cannot understand anything the student says. However, upon being shown a summary of the student's presentation, the professors realize that they have understood most of it.

• *Ask the student to spell a word or rephrase a statement.* Students do not like this as much and often say that after two attempts they quit trying to answer, but it is sometimes effective.

• *Have the students write on the board.* This is only effective in smaller classes and if international students are not the only students singled out. Ask American students to write on the board also.

• *Have another student rephrase the question.* If the students feel comfortable in the class, they will often turn to a fellow student and ask for assistance, or a fellow student will "interpret." However, this will probably occur only in a class with predominately international students because they are then less embarrassed by poor communication skills.

3. *Give students time to reflect.* Many Americans think aloud, but people from many other cultures do not. What this means is that international students rarely have time to reflect and respond before an American student or the professor has taken over the conversation. In Finland it is not unusual for a student to take fifteen to twenty seconds before responding to a professor's question. To an American professor accustomed to five-second responses, this can seem like an eternity.

Give your students enough time to respond; allow thinking time. International students have frequently been taught not to speak in class unless what they have to say is important or they have thought through the question. Americans, accustomed to the five-second response, feel uncomfortable with the silence and begin a response by thinking aloud. International students feel as uncomfortable with the thinking aloud concept as you do when you must wait twenty seconds to respond.

Vocabulary

International students express concern about the prevalence of idioms and slang in newspaper and magazine articles as well as in speech. Many of the students have a sufficient discipline-specific vocabulary when they arrive in the United States. However, idiomatic terms and slang are rarely taught overseas, and this causes students great difficulty. Some of the terms students need explained include such idioms as *bottom line, getting orders right and left,* and *wear and tear.* These seem simple to native speakers, but they are traps for language learners. So what can you, the professor, do? Student recommendations include the following:

1. *Try to avoid idiomatic language and slang.* Listen carefully to what you say. If you use idioms, slang, or long series of adjectives or nouns, repeat the concept in more academic terms. For example, *can* and *can't* sound remarkably similar in conversational English but totally change the meaning of a sentence. International students report that in the classroom, it is often easier for them to hear and understand the professors than their peers. Accordingly, you should consider repeating peer comments or questions, particularly when idiomatic language or slang is used.

Proverbs can also create problems for international students. In explaining Federal Reserve policies, one professor used the proverb "You can lead a horse to water, but you can't make him drink." The student had absolutely no idea what the professor meant until the proverb was explained.

2. *Write key terms and vocabulary on the board.* Sentence stress is extremely important in spoken English, and it is often difficult for a non-native speaker to distinguish stressed words in a sentence from the syllable stress in specific words. Students describing this difficulty state that having professors write important terms, vocabulary, and concepts on the board helps them grasp important points in the lecture.

Writing

International students recognize writing as a problem that will plague most of them throughout their academic careers. The suggestions that the students have made are valid. The following suggestions provide a starting point for the improvement of writing skills.

1. *Provide models.* By providing students—international and American—with samples of both good and bad papers or assignments, the students can begin to decipher the assignment and analyze your criteria for an acceptable paper.

2. *Explain in simple but detailed terms what you expect.* Writing styles vary from country to country, and international students may not be aware of what is expected for an academic paper in the United States. For instance, a Taiwanese student received a failing grade on a project because she misunderstood the requirements. She thought that she had to invent an entirely new

strategy rather than relate the project to the textbooks and lectures. The professor could have reinforced the requirements by reminding her what the details of the project were.

Conclusion

All of the problems identified by the students can be solved, and the students themselves have provided some practical beginnings that can help you ease their transition to U.S. academic life. Student-perceived issues do not always match educator-perceived issues; nevertheless, eliciting information from the students allows them to become part of the solution.

DEBRA S. LEE is an ESL instructor at the University of Augsburg School of Law in Germany. She has also taught EFL in Finland and ESL at the University of Memphis.

INDEX